Heinemann EXPLORE Science

Teacher's Book

New International Edition

Grade 5

Tara Lievesley, Deborah Herridge
Series editor: John Stringer

ALWAYS LEARNING

PEARSON

Pearson Education Limited is a company incorporated in England and Wales having its registered office at Edinburgh Gate, Harlow, Essex, CM20 2JE.

Registered company number: 872828

Text © Pearson Education Limited 2012
First published 2003
This edition published 2012

www.pearsonglobalschools.com

16 15 14 13 12
IMP 10 9 8 7 6 5 4 3 2 1

British Library Cataloguing in Publication Data
A catalogue record for this book is available from the British Library

ISBN 978 0 43513 367 2

Copyright notice

Edited by Glenys Davis
Produced by Tech-Set Ltd, Gateshead
Original illustrations © Pearson Education Limited, 2003, 2009, 2012
Illustrated by Tech-Set Ltd, Gateshead
Cover photo/illustration © Alamy Images
Printed in China (SWTC/01)

Acknowledgements
Every effort has been made to contact copyright holders of material reproduced in this book. Any omissions will be rectified in subsequent printings if notice is given to the publishers.

Contents   **Grade 5**

G4
Heating & cooling

Introduction   1

Unit 1: Microbes   **16**

Microbes and you   18

Investigating microbes   20

Using microbes   22

Unit 1: Review   24

Unit 2: Keeping healthy   **26**

Keeping fit   28

Your heart   30

Pumping blood   32

Counting heartbeats   34

Investigating pulse rate   36

Drugs and you   38

Unit 2: Review   40

Unit 3: Life cycles   **42**

The Sun's light   44

New life   46

Fruits and seeds   48

Investigating seed shapes   50

Germinating seeds   52

Life cycles   54

Unit 3: Review   56

Unit 4: Light   **58**

Light sources   60

Blackout blinds   62

Changing shadows   64

Sunlight and shadows   66

How we see things   68

Reflection   70

Unit 4: Review   72

Unit 5: Changing state   **74**

Evaporation   76

Investigating evaporation   78

Graphing evaporation   80

Condensation   82

Investigating boiling and freezing   84

The water cycle   86

Unit 5: Review   88

Unit 6: The Earth and beyond   **90**

Our solar system   92

The Earth, Sun and Moon   94

Our turning Earth   96

Astronomers   98

Night and day   100

The Moon   102

The passing year   104

Unit 6: Review   106

iii

New International Edition

Introduction

Heinemann Explore Science *New International Edition* provides a comprehensive, easy-to-use resource written especially for the international primary classroom.

The teaching framework follows the Cambridge International Examinations Primary Science Curriculum Framework (2011), enabling you to minimize planning. The simple structure of ***Heinemann Explore Science*** gives you flexibility to teach the Units within a Grade in the order that suits your situation.

There is one Unit for each half of a term, with multiple lessons in that Unit. The first lesson in each Unit is an introduction and the last one is a plenary. The other lessons either focus on knowledge and understanding or on manageable, tried and tested investigation activities. The greater the opportunity for investigation, the more practical lessons there are.

Each Grade of ***Heinemann Explore Science*** contains in the *Teacher's Book* detailed teacher's notes, which provide all the resources you need for planning and delivering successful science lessons. It also includes an accompanying *Student Book* to bring the science topics to life for the children; a *Workbook* with activities to do at school or at home, and six *Readers* to develop students' English language skills through science. Alongside these components, digital resources available via online subscription provide an e-book version of the printed books, opportunities for independent research into the Biology, Chemistry and Physics covered in the scheme and further activities and simulations. For more information on digital resources for this course, visit www.pearsonglobalschools.com/explorescience.

This unique combination of science and ICT stimulates students and enables you to deliver enriching science lessons using today's technology.

Heinemann Explore Science and English language development

Science and language development have much in common. In both, students are frequently highly motivated. Science is a popular subject area in primary schools with students (and with teachers!), and produces interesting and engaging results. Language and science are both social activities. Students' language will not develop without co-operation and collaboration, and science is also a collaborative subject. Finally, science experiences can lead, as few other subjects do, to a desire to communicate discoveries.

When developing spoken English, remember:

- Discussion can be stimulated by working in threes. Two friends doing science may have a common and familiar way of communicating. Three extends the discussion.

- Snowball or jigsaw activities, in which groups share and exchange information, are engaging.

- Discussion before and after an investigation can clarify thoughts. Having to explain what students discovered in their investigation helps clarify thinking and improve language skills.

- Presenting results to others imposes a discipline as well as giving purpose to recording and to clear presentation.

- Reading can be developed through following instructions – including safety instructions – and using the *Student Book* and targeted *Readers*.

Students may be understandably reluctant to record their discoveries. When encouraging written recording, use a variety of recording methods.

- Writing to a structure helps to order students' thoughts.

- Annotated diagrams are an effective way of recording practical science – used by adult scientists as well as students.

- A recorded observation alone may lead to a conclusion.

- Ordering and recording whole investigations is difficult, and can often be better done to a writing framework.

Heinemann Explore Science offers and defines new vocabulary. If the words are new to you, or you have any doubts yourself about their definition, use the definitions in the Glossary in the *Student Book*.

- Draw the students' attention to the new words.

- Depending on the students' age, set them to illustrate or define the words themselves. Introduce word games – matching the word to the definition.

- Make a 'Words of Science' poster or a class dictionary.

- Ask the students to use the words in context; to act them out; to guess which word you are thinking of, either by 20 questions or by giving clues.
- Use cloze procedure to place new words.

Components of the scheme

The **Heinemann Explore Science** *Teacher's Book* provides detailed guidance on teaching with the corresponding sections of the *Student Book* pages. Used alongside the electronic components, where you will find a variety of resources for planning and teaching, the *Teacher's Book* is the main starting point for any lesson. Each Unit provides approximately a half-term's worth of work – an introduction, and almost always four lesson plans (each of which may be taught in a single session or across science sessions during the week), and a final review.

Each Unit introduction provides:

1 Clear background science information to support the non-specialist teacher.

2 Simple definitions of necessary scientific vocabulary.

3 A complete list of resources needed in the Unit.

4 Helpful hints on prior preparation or useful additional resources.

5 Indications of what students should already know and be able to do before starting the Unit.

6 Cross-curricular references to other subject areas.

7 A discussion question to set the scene and introduce a context for the Unit.

There are two types of lesson in **Heinemann Explore Science**. The first type focuses on knowledge and understanding objectives. These lessons contain:

1 Starter activities to initiate whole-class discussion. Questioning will enable you to establish what the students already know.

2 References to the corresponding *Student Book* pages and further information to expand on the paragraphs in the *Student Book*.

3 Safety tips to advise of specific hazards where appropriate.

4 Additional information necessary for the activities in the 'Things to do' section of the *Student Book*, plus suggestions of how to differentiate and record. Any worksheets required are cross-referenced.

5 Integrated ICT research activities using the website.

6 Further details or extra 'fun facts' to support those listed in the *Student Book*.

7 The answer to the 'I wonder...' question, with additional background explanation if necessary.

8 More activities that can be used instead of, or as well as, those in the 'Things to do' section.

9 Ideas for how students could present their work or tips for classroom displays are provided on the website to help students.

10 Suggestions for homework activities.

11 An activity or series of questions to reinforce the main objectives in the plenary session, drawing the lesson to a close.

The second type of lesson offers a challenge to encourage students to use scientific enquiry skills to investigate a problem in context. These contain:

1 Starter activities to initiate whole-class discussion.

2 A challenge introduced in context, explaining what students will be investigating.

3 Safety tips advising of unique hazards where appropriate; an individual risk assessment is always recommended.

4 Further details of how to carry out the investigation, supporting the instructions in the *Student Book*.

5 Lists of materials students will need, including any to be prepared in advance.

6 Explanations of what students should be looking for, or how to keep the test fair. How best to support and extend students.

7 How to organize, record, analyze and present data collected in the investigation. Suitable tables for data recording are provided as worksheets in the *Workbook*.

8 Students are encouraged to review how well they carried out their investigation and how good their results were. Using the report provided for each investigation helps students build evaluation skills by criticizing methods and conclusions.

9   A different scenario is offered to enable students to apply what they have learned.

10 Additional activities can be used instead of, or as well as, the investigative challenge.

11 Suggestions for homework activities.

12 An activity or series of questions to reinforce the main objectives in the plenary session draw the lesson to a close.

At the end of each Unit, material is provided for an assessment and review lesson:

1   A clear summary of the knowledge and skills students have gained through the Unit divided into three levels of attainment.

2   Explanation and expected responses to the 'Check-up' in the *Student Book*.

3   Answers to the assessment worksheets in the *Workbook*.

4   The answer to the original question posed at the beginning of the Unit.

5   A final activity completes the Unit and reminds students of everything they have learned.

In addition, there are six readers for each Grade of the Framework. These are written to match the appropriate science for the Grade, but with close attention to language levels. Students can learn English language through science, and science through practising their English.

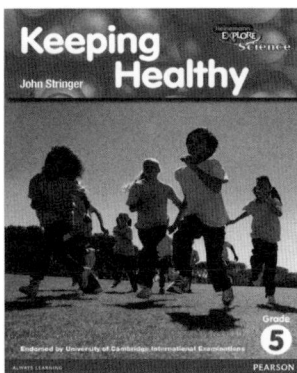

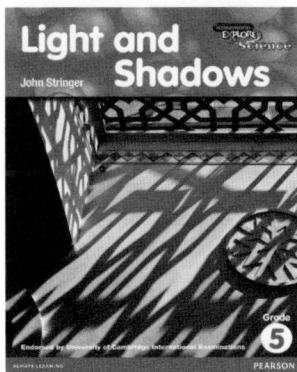

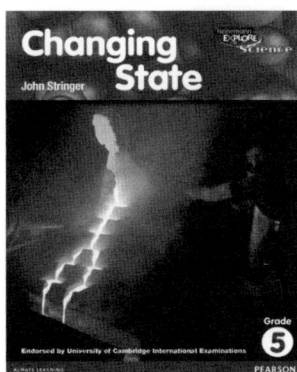

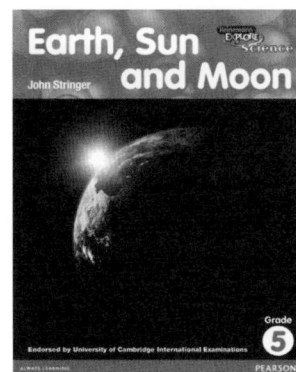

Keeping Healthy

Life Cycles

Light and Shadows

How We See Things

Changing State

Earth, Sun and Moon

New International Edition

Quick guide to the *Teacher's Book*

The ***Heinemann Explore Science*** *Grade 5 Teacher's Book* provides detailed guidance on teaching with the corresponding sections of the *Student Book* pages. Used alongside the e-book, the *Teacher's Book* is the main starting point for any lesson. Each Unit provides approximately one half-term's worth of work and comprises an introduction and generally six or seven lessons (each of which may be taught all at once, or across a number of science sessions during the week), plus a review.

Each Unit introduction provides:

2 A complete list of resources needed throughout the Unit.

3 Helpful hints on prior preparation or useful resources.

1 Clear background science information to support the non-specialist teacher.

4 Indicators of what students should know and be able to do before starting this Unit.

7 Useful definitions of scientific vocabulary commonly misunderstood by students.

5 Specific references to other subject areas.

6 An initial discussion question to set the scene and introduce a context for the Unit.

There are two types of lesson in *Heinemann Explore Science*. The first type focuses on knowledge and understanding objectives.

1 Starter activities initiate whole-class discussion. Questioning will enable you to find out what the students already know.

2 Safety tips warn of possible hazards where appropriate.

3 The answer to the 'I wonder...' question, with additional background explanations if necessary.

10 Any additional information necessary for the activities in the 'Things to do' section of the *Student Book*, plus suggestions of how to differentiate and record.

4 Ideas for how students could present their work or tips for classroom displays.

9 References to the corresponding *Student Book* pages and further information to expand on the paragraphs in the *Student Book*.

5 Suggestions for homework activities.

8 Further details or extra 'fun facts' to support those listed in the *Student Book*.

7 More activities that can be used instead of or as well as those in the 'Things to do' section.

6 An activity or series of questions to help reinforce the main objectives in the Plenary session to draw the lesson to a close.

The second type of lesson offers a challenge to encourage students to use their scientific enquiry skills to investigate a problem in context.

1 Starter activities initiate whole-class discussion.

2 Safety tips warn of possible hazards where appropriate.

3 Information on how to organize, record, analyze and present data collected in the investigation. Tables for recording results and exemplar data to convert into charts or graphs can be found in the *Student Book* and *Workbook*.

4 Presents students with a different scenario to enable them to apply what they have learned.

5 More activities that can be used instead of or as well as the investigative challenge.

6 Suggestions for homework activities.

7 An activity or series of questions to help reinforce the main objectives in the plenary session to draw the lesson to a close.

8 Students are encouraged to review how well they carried out their investigation and how good their results were. Use the report provided for each investigation to help students build evaluation skills by criticizing methods and conclusions.

9 Explanations of what students should be looking for and noticing, or how they should keep the test fair. Ideas on how to support and extend students are also included.

10 List of materials that students will need, including any that need to be prepared in advance.

11 Further details of how to carry out the investigation to support the instructions to the students in the *Student Book*.

12 The challenge introduces the context and explains what students will be investigating.

At the end of each Unit, material is provided for an assessment and review lesson.

1 A clear summary of the knowledge and skills students should have gained throughout the Unit.

2 Assessment sheets can be found in the *Workbook* and e-book.

3 A final activity completes the Unit to remind students of everything they have learned.

4 The answer to the original question posed at the beginning of the Unit. Discuss what the students think now in light of what they have learned.

5 Explanation and expected responses to the Check-up in the *Student Book*.

How to use *Heinemann Explore Science*

For ease of use, ***Heinemann Explore Science*** follows the structure of the Cambridge Primary Science Curriculum Framework, 2011. ***Heinemann Explore Science*** has been written so that you can be flexible about what you teach and when.

Heinemann Explore Science is more manageable than many primary science schemes. It has a simple structure, but it also offers wide investigative and research opportunities. A range of engaging tasks is offered for each topic, including practical and research-based activities. Its clear progression and layout offers more support to less confident teachers. Integrated assessment gives indications of how to interpret levels of attainment. There is support for differentiation with suggestions for extra challenges for bright students and support for students struggling with science concepts. There is both experimental and investigative science through reliable practical investigations.

Heinemann Explore Science emphasizes: investigations; the clear use of strong vocabulary lists; building on students' ideas and addressing common misconceptions through questioning and discussion; clearly identified support and extend activities; class demonstration as a basis for some practical activities; and appropriate activities as part of students' homework. It offers flexibility of use; although Units are ordered to match the Cambridge Curriculum Framework, they can be taught in any order to suit a school's own scheme of work. This helps in mixed-age classes.

Differentiation

Within any class there will be a wide range of experience and ability. In a mixed-age class that range is further extended. This is a challenge to any teacher, and many address it through careful differentiation. Commonly, work is planned for a number of different groups (often three: high achievers, a middle range group, and students needing additional support). Teachers then allocate their resources – human and practical – to these groups to ensure the best possible outcome for everybody. This 'planning for differentiation'

is demanding, and may leave feelings of dissatisfaction – 'I didn't spend long enough with the high-fliers/slower group today', 'I hope I'm not neglecting the majority of the class'. Some teachers have similar difficulties with 'differentiation by outcome'. Less able students may be unchallenged by the assumption that they will always produce a few lines of text when others routinely write a page.

Heinemann Explore Science expects that you will need to differentiate your work, and so a range of resources is offered, any of which may stimulate particular groups. You may choose to: present an activity on an investigation table, possibly supported by an informed adult; to set out resources that students can use for creative play; or to use the *Student Book* or *Workbook* for stimulus, for direction or for recording.

The 'starting off' activities in ***Heinemann Explore Science*** invite a third form of differentiation: differentiation by presentation. This is so familiar to teachers that few recognize how effectively they use it. The way in which a topic is presented engages students, but it also enables you to assess their prior knowledge. Because of its practical nature, students who may not shine in other subjects will often contribute more in science. Students who are able in every respect may still surprise you with their knowledge, but this 'knowledge' needs to be probed carefully – a superficial knowledge may lack the depth of understanding on which new science learning can be built.

That's why ***Heinemann Explore Science*** includes a number of exemplar questions to elicit current understanding – whether it is insecure, or even whether students have misconceptions that need gently challenging. It is when you group the students and set the tasks that you 'differentiate by presentation' – an unconscious and instinctive skill that results in different groups busily engaged with differing levels of support and monitoring.

Level statements to help you identify at which level students are working are provided in this *Teacher's Book*, for each Unit. These are also provided at the back of the *Student Book* for discussion and as checklists to enable self-assessment by students.

Heinemann Explore Science contains a wide range of ideas for interaction that includes things to do, questions to ask and resources to support learning. Your professional role is in the effective deployment of those resources.

The Heinemann Explore Science website

This provides a full range of editable planning materials, generic writing frames and presentation templates to support students in recording and presenting their work.

The website also provides digital e-book versions of all the *Readers* for each Grade and for the *Student Books* and *Workbooks*, so that worksheets can be downloaded and printed if needed.

Using ICT for research

Students should develop their research skills using a variety of secondary sources. Throughout the *Student Book*, students are given opportunities to use ICT to research the answers to questions related to the topic of the lesson. At the end of each Unit, a more open question with reference only to the appropriate area of study is introduced to encourage students to develop search skills and strategies.

The Heinemann Explore Science Readers

These have been written bearing in mind the language needs of students for whom English is not a first language. Each book complements a Unit in the scheme. They offer interesting illustrations and simple, engaging text. Word count increases with higher Grades. They can be used as individual readers, books to read at home, or for group reading. They can be used for vocabulary and language exercise, and there are suggestions for activities at the back of each book – from crosswords to team games.

Used alongside the other components of the scheme, they offer opportunities for developing science and language, hand in hand.

Health and safety issues

Primary science is a very safe activity, but that does not mean that you should not consider health and safety issues when you plan, or that you should feel unsupported, either. *Heinemann Explore Science* highlights specific safety issues in lessons when appropriate, and you should also engage in your own risk assessment and take appropriate precautions. This should not be demanding; it involves looking at your students, your circumstances and support staff, and ensuring that you have noted, minimized and if necessary recorded any apparent hazards. It is essential to share this risk assessment with other adults in the classroom.

Every adult on the school site should be familiar with the school's Health and Safety Policy, and especially how it reflects on their responsibilities. They should know the location and proper use of safety equipment. All adults have a responsibility for their own safety, and that of their students in school, whatever their age. This is a responsibility you share with others. Teaching assistants, for example, are often responsible for small groups of students doing practical activities – their supervision may be vital where a hazard has been recognized, for example, when using a cooker. Working with a small group like this offers opportunities not just for realistic but negative teaching ('Don't touch that – it's hot!') but also for positive modelling of safe behaviour ('Now how should I pick this up?').

You can give a very positive image of health and safety issues by performing a routine risk assessment while planning an activity, and encouraging students to make their own assessment of risk, and take their own precautions. Engaging students in safety planning helps them to understand the importance of not taking risks. If students are simply told what is safe without explanation they are less likely to take it as seriously as when they are themselves involved in safety planning.

Here are a few general common-sense reminders:

Food: Eating and drinking is forbidden in school science labs, but some of primary science is concerned with food – science activities may require students to eat, but only with your permission. Fingers do get sucked, and foods are tempting. Ensure that guidelines on 'what to eat' are clear and take into account ethnicity, custom, parental wishes and allergies.

7

Present the best practice in food handling: the cleaning and/or covering of tables, and the use of cooking utensils kept only for this purpose. Pupils should know not to enter the food area unless they are in the practical group (mark or point out an area that can only be entered with clean hands and wearing an apron). Protective clothing not only keeps the students' clothes clean but also prevents food contamination. It should be kept solely for food use. PVC aprons or smocks (coveralls) can be cleaned by wiping with an antibacterial cleaner. Washable aprons should be hot washed at least once a term.

Laminated plastic tables are ideal. Wooden tables (or damaged laminated tables) should be covered with clean plastic tablecloths kept specifically for food. Older students can use antibacterial cleaners after an initial thorough clean by an adult. Spray or wipe all food preparation surfaces including chopping boards with the antibacterial cleaner, wipe clean and leave to dry before using.

Nobody – pupil or adult – should work with food if they are unwell, including sickness, diarrhoea, colds, coughs and other infections. Cuts must be covered with a clean waterproof dressing – blue plasters show up if they drop into food! Supervise students washing hands before food work, or after using the toilet. Provide colourless, perfume-free liquid soap and running water. If a hot air dryer is not available, provide disposable paper towels or paper roller towels. Discourage students from touching their face, hair or other parts of their body, and from coughing or sneezing over food.

Electricity: Teach students about the dangers of mains electricity. Students live with electricity and refusing them experience of it is comparable to not teaching them road safety rules for fear of traffic accidents. Mains electricity has a far greater 'push' round the circuit than battery electricity. It is this greater push that kills. The human body is not a good conductor of electricity, but it conducts electricity far better when wet. Work with low-voltage 'battery' electricity is not risky.

Forces: Many activities in science (and technology) put students at risk because little thought is given to possible outcomes. What will happen if the elastic band snaps, the bag breaks, or the liquid spills? Students may take unnecessary risks too, by not using basic science equipment (eye protection, a cutting board or bench hook)

that could keep them safe. Testing-to-breaking-point activities in topics such as Forces can be dangerous unless students have considered the consequences of breakage.

Animals: The key factor is the welfare of both students and animals. The learning outcome is an understanding of animal welfare and a positive educational experience of (say) a small mammal. It's important to ensure that none of the students has an allergy to animal fur. If you introduce family pets, it's unlikely that they are used to being surrounded by a group of excited students.

Introduce any animal to a group/class yourself. Talk about them, drawing out what the students know, and what they think about how the animal might behave. Students empathize with small animals, and will understand that they could be easily frightened.

The adult should handle the animal throughout the group activity. Students could ask their questions first, and then take it in turns to stroke the animal at the end, which reduces the chances that students will go rubbing their eyes or sucking their fingers afterwards! After their experience, they should wash their hands again, under supervision.

General advice: Younger students can be expected to be able to control risks to themselves and others. They commonly know what is dangerous. Classroom accidents are frequently the result of students forgetting what is sensible because they are caught up in an activity, especially if it is exciting science!

Essential safety advice is contained in a book from the Association for Science Education called *'Be Safe!'* and every teacher should be aware of it and its contents. *Be Safe!* is available from The Association for Science Education, College Lane, Hatfield, Herts. AL10 9AA, UK

www.ase.org.uk
Be Safe! ISBN: 978 0 86357 426 9

CLEAPSS is the advisory service for health and safety in science education. CLEAPSS offers informative publications, a staffed helpline, and a members' website. It is an essential source of science safety knowledge.

www.cleapss.org.uk

Curriculum structure of *Heinemann Explore Science*

Heinemann Explore Science has been very carefully structured to ensure a progressive development in the students using the course, both of scientific process skills and also of knowledge and understanding. This complements the approach taken in the Cambridge Primary Science Curriculum Framework.

The development of scientific process skills throughout the complete course is shown in this skills ladder:

Heinemann Explore Science Science Skills Ladder

Skills Domain	Year 1 Children have opportunities:	Year 2 Children have opportunities:	Year 3 Children have opportunities:	Year 4 Children have opportunities:	Year 5 Children have opportunities:	Year 6 Children have opportunities:
1. Ideas and evidence in science	to collect evidence to try to answer a question	to collect evidence to try to answer a question	to collect evidence in a variety of contexts to answer a question or test an idea	to collect evidence in a variety of contexts to test an idea or prediction based on their scientific knowledge and understanding	to consider how scientists have combined evidence from observation and measurement with creative thinking to suggest new ideas and explanations for phenomena	to consider how scientists have combined evidence from observation and measurement with creative thinking to suggest new ideas and explanations for phenomena
2. Investigative skills **Planning investigative work**	to test ideas suggested to them and say what they think will happen	to suggest some ideas and questions based on simple knowledge and say how they might find out about them; to say what they think might happen; and to think about and discuss whether comparisons and tests are fair or unfair	in a variety of contexts, to suggest questions and ideas and how to test them; to make predictions about what will happen; to think about how to collect sufficient evidence in some contexts; and to consider what makes a test unfair or evidence sufficient and, with help, plan fair tests	to suggest questions that can be tested and make predictions about what will happen, some of which are based on scientific knowledge; to design a fair test or plan how to collect sufficient evidence; and, in some contexts, to choose what apparatus to use and what to measure	to make predictions of what will happen based on scientific knowledge and understanding, and suggest how to test these; to use knowledge and understanding to plan how to carry out a fair test or how to collect sufficient evidence to test an idea; and to identify factors that need to be taken into consideration in different contexts	to decide how to turn ideas into a form that can be tested and, where appropriate, to make predictions using scientific knowledge and understanding; to identify factors that are relevant to a particular situation; to choose what evidence to collect to investigate a question, ensuring the evidence is sufficient; and to choose what equipment to use

New International Edition

Heinemann Explore Science Science Skills Ladder

Skills Domain	Year 1 Children have opportunities:	Year 2 Children have opportunities:	Year 3 Children have opportunities:	Year 4 Children have opportunities:	Year 5 Children have opportunities:	Year 6 Children have opportunities:
3. Obtaining and presenting evidence		to make observations using appropriate senses; to make some measurements of length using standard and non-standard measures; and to present some findings in simple tables and block graphs	to make observations and comparisons; to measure length, volume of liquid and time in standard measures using simple measuring equipment effectively; and to present results in drawing, bar charts and tables	to make observations and comparisons of relevant features in a variety of contexts; to make measurements of temperature, time and force as well as measurements of length; to begin to think about why measurements of length should be repeated; and to present results in bar charts and tables	to make relevant observations; to consolidate measurement of volume, temperature, time and length; to measure pulse rate; to think about why observations and measurements should be repeated; and to present results in bar charts and line graphs	to make a variety of relevant observations and measurements using simple apparatus correctly; to decide when observations and measurements need to be checked, by repeating, to give more reliable data; and to use tables, bar charts and line graphs to present results
4. Considering evidence and approach	to communicate observations orally, in drawing, by labelling and in simple writing; to make simple comparisons and groupings that relate to differences and similarities between living things and objects; in some cases to say what their observations show, and whether it was what they expected; and to draw simple conclusions and explain what they did	to make simple comparisons, identifying similarities and differences between living things, objects and events; to say what results show; to say whether their predictions were supported; in some cases to use knowledge to explain what was found out and to draw conclusions; and to explain what they did	to draw conclusions from results and begin to use scientific knowledge to suggest explanations for them; and to make generalizations and begin to identify simple patterns in results presented in tables	to identify simple trends and patterns in results presented in tables, charts and graphs and to suggest explanations for some of these; to explain what the evidence shows and whether it supports any predictions made; and to link the evidence to scientific knowledge and understanding in some contexts	to decide whether results support any prediction; to begin to evaluate repeated results; to recognize and make predictions from patterns in data and suggest explanations for these using scientific knowledge and understanding; to interpret data and think about whether it is sufficient to draw conclusions; and to draw conclusions indicating whether these match any prediction made	to make comparisons; to evaluate repeated results; to identify patterns in results and results that do not appear to fit the pattern; to use results to draw conclusions and to make further predictions; to suggest and evaluate explanations for these predictions using scientific knowledge and understanding; and to say whether the evidence supports any prediction made

Heinemann Explore Science Curriculum Matching Chart for Grade 5

This chart shows where all of the topics and Learning Objectives specified in the Cambridge Primary Science Curriculum Framework are covered in the *Heinemann Explore Science* course.

Learning Objectives	Student Book coverage	Supporting coverage in Teacher's Book or Workbook
Scientific enquiry		
Scientific enquiry: Ideas and evidence		
Know that scientists have combined evidence with creative thinking to suggest new ideas and explanations for phenomena.	Unit 3: Life cycles • Fruits and seeds pp.28–9 Unit 6: The Earth and beyond • Our solar system pp.66–7 • Astronomers pp.72–3	Teacher's Book 5, pp.42–57 Teacher's Book 5, pp.90–107
Use observation and measurement to test predictions and make links.	Unit 1: Microbes • Investigating microbes pp.4–5 • Using microbes pp.6–7 Unit 2: Keeping healthy • Investigating pulse rate pp.18–19 Unit 3: Life cycles • Investigating seed shapes pp.30–1 Unit 4: Light • Blackout blinds pp.40–1 • Changing shadows pp.42–3 Unit 5: Changing state • Investigating evaporation pp.54–5 • Graphing evaporation pp.56–7 • Investigating boiling and freezing pp.60–1 Unit 6: The Earth and beyond • Our turning Earth pp.70–1	Teacher's Book 5, pp.16–25 Teacher's Book 5, pp.26–41 Teacher's Book 5, pp.42–57 Teacher's Book 5, pp.58–73 Teacher's Book 5, pp.74–89 Teacher's Book 5, pp.90–107
Scientific enquiry: Plan investigative work		
Make predictions of what will happen based on scientific knowledge and understanding, and suggest and communicate how to test these.	Unit 1: Microbes • Investigating microbes pp.4–5 • Using microbes pp.6–7 Unit 2: Keeping healthy • Investigating pulse rate pp.18–19 Unit 3: Life cycles • Investigating seed shapes pp.30–1 Unit 4: Light • Blackout blinds pp.40–1 • Changing shadows pp.42–3 • Sunlight and shadows pp.44–5 Unit 5: Changing state • Investigating evaporation pp.54–5 • Graphing evaporation pp.56–7 • Investigating boiling and freezing pp.60–1 Unit 6: The Earth and beyond • Our turning Earth pp.70–1	Teacher's Book 5, pp.16–25 Teacher's Book 5, pp.26–41 Teacher's Book 5, pp.42–57 Teacher's Book 5, pp.58–73 Teacher's Book 5, pp.74–89 Teacher's Book 5, pp.90–107
Use knowledge and understanding to plan how to carry out a fair test.	Unit 3: Life cycles • Germinating seeds pp.32–3 Unit 5: Changing state • Graphing evaporation pp.56–7	Teacher's Book 5, pp.42–57 Teacher's Book 5, pp.74–89
Collect sufficient evidence to test an idea.	Unit 1: Microbes • Microbes and you pp.2–3 Unit 3: Life cycles • Fruits and seeds pp.28–9 • Investigating seed shapes pp.30–1 Unit 5: Changing state • Graphing evaporation pp.56–7 Unit 6: The Earth and beyond • Our solar system pp.66–7	Teacher's Book 5, pp.16–25 Teacher's Book 5, pp.42–57 Teacher's Book 5, pp.74–89 Teacher's Book 5, pp.90–107

11

Identify factors that need to be taken into account in different contexts.	Unit 1: Microbes • Investigating microbes pp.4–5	*Teacher's Book* 5, pp.16–25
	Unit 3: Life cycles • Investigating seed shapes pp.30–1 • Germinating seeds pp.32–3	*Teacher's Book* 5, pp.42–57
	Unit 4: Light • Sunlight and shadows pp.44–5	*Teacher's Book* 5, pp.58–73
	Unit 5: Changing state • Investigating evaporation pp.54–5 • Graphing evaporation pp.56–7	*Teacher's Book* 5, pp.74–89
	Unit 6: The Earth and beyond • Our turning Earth pp.70–1	*Teacher's Book* 5, pp.90–107

Scientific enquiry: Obtain and present evidence

Make relevant observations.	Unit 1: Microbes • Investigating microbes pp.4–5	*Teacher's Book* 5, pp.16–25
	Unit 3: Life cycles • Fruits and seeds pp.28–9 • Investigating seed shapes pp.30–1	*Teacher's Book* 5, pp.42–57
	Unit 4: Light • Changing shadows pp.42–3 • Sunlight and shadows pp.44–5	*Teacher's Book* 5, pp.58–73
	Unit 5: Changing state • Evaporation pp.52–3	*Teacher's Book* 5, pp.74–89
Measure volume, temperature, time, length and force.	Unit 3: Life cycles • Investigating seed shapes pp.30–1	*Teacher's Book* 5, pp.42–57
	Unit 4: Light • Sunlight and shadows pp.44–5	*Teacher's Book* 5, pp.58–73
	Unit 5: Changing state • Investigating evaporation pp.54–5 • Graphing evaporation pp.56–7 • Investigating boiling and freezing pp.60–1	*Teacher's Book* 5, pp.74–89
Discuss the need for repeated observations and measurements.	Unit 1: Microbes • Investigating microbes pp.4–5	*Teacher's Book* 5, pp.16–25
	Unit 2: Keeping healthy • Investigating pulse rate pp.18–19	*Teacher's Book* 5, pp.26–41
	Unit 3: Life cycles • Investigating seed shapes pp.30–1	*Teacher's Book* 5, pp.42–57
	Unit 4: Light • Blackout blinds pp.40–1	*Teacher's Book* 5, pp.58–73
	Unit 5: Changing state • Investigating evaporation pp.54–5	*Teacher's Book* 5, pp.74–89
Present results in bar charts and line graphs.	Unit 1: Microbes • Investigating microbes pp.4–5	*Teacher's Book* 5, pp.16–25
	Unit 2: Keeping healthy • Investigating pulse rate pp.18–19	*Teacher's Book* 5, pp.26–41
	Unit 3: Life cycles • Investigating seed shapes pp.30–1 • Germinating seeds pp.32–3	*Teacher's Book* 5, pp.42–57
	Unit 5: Changing state • Investigating boiling and freezing pp.60–1	*Teacher's Book* 5, pp.74–89

Scientific enquiry: Consider evidence and approach

Decide whether results support predictions.	Unit 2: Keeping healthy • Investigating pulse rate pp.18–19	*Teacher's Book* 5, pp.26–41
	Unit 3: Life cycles • Investigating seed shapes pp.30–31	*Teacher's Book* 5, pp.42–57
	Unit 4: Light • Blackout blinds pp.40–41 • Changing shadows pp.42–43	*Teacher's Book* 5, pp.58–73
	Unit 6: The Earth and beyond • Our turning Earth pp.70–71	*Teacher's Book* 5, pp.90–107

Begin to evaluate repeated results.	Unit 5: Changing state • Investigating evaporation pp.54–5	*Teacher's Book* 5, pp.74–89
Recognize and make predictions from patterns in data and suggest explanations using scientific knowledge and understanding.	Unit 1: Microbes • Investigating microbes pp.4–5	*Teacher's Book* 5, pp.16–25
	Unit 2: Keeping healthy • Counting heartbeats pp.16–17	*Teacher's Book* 5, pp.26–41
	Unit 3: Life cycles • Investigating seed shapes pp.30–1	*Teacher's Book* 5, pp.42–57
	Unit 4: Light • Sunlight and shadows pp.44–5	*Teacher's Book* 5, pp.58–73
	Unit 5: Changing state • Investigating boiling and freezing pp.60–1	*Teacher's Book* 5, pp.74–89
	Unit 6: The Earth and beyond • Night and day pp.74–5	*Teacher's Book* 5, pp.90–107
Interpret data and think about whether it is sufficient to draw conclusions.	Unit 3: Life cycles • Germinating seeds pp.32–3	*Teacher's Book* 5, pp.42–57
	Unit 6: The Earth and beyond • Our turning Earth pp.70–1	*Teacher's Book* 5, pp.90–107

Biology

Biology: Plants

Know that plants need energy from light for growth.	Unit 3: Life cycles • The Sun's light pp.24–5	*Teacher's Book* 5, pp.42–57
Know that plants reproduce.	Unit 3: Life cycles • New life pp.26–7	*Teacher's Book* 5, pp.42–57
Observe how seeds can be dispersed in a variety of ways.	Unit 3: Life cycles • Fruits and seeds pp.28–9	*Teacher's Book* 5, pp.42–57
Investigate how seeds need water and warmth for germination, but not light.	Unit 3: Life cycles • Germinating seeds pp.32–3	*Teacher's Book* 5, pp.42–57
Know that insects pollinate some flowers.	Unit 3: Life cycles • New life pp.26–7	*Teacher's Book* 5, pp.42–57
Observe that plants produce flowers which have male and female organs; seeds are formed when pollen from the male organ fertilizes the ovum (female).	Unit 3: Life cycles • New life pp.26–7	*Teacher's Book* 5, pp.42–57
Recognize that flowering plants have a life cycle including pollination, fertilization, seed production, seed dispersal and germination.	Unit 3: Life cycles • Life cycles pp.34–5	*Teacher's Book* 5, pp.42–57 *Workbook* 5, p.9

Chemistry

Chemistry: States of matter

Know that evaporation occurs when a liquid turns into a gas.	Unit 5: Changing state • Evaporation pp.52–3 • Investigating evaporation pp.54–5 • Graphing evaporation pp.56–7	*Teacher's Book* 5, pp.74–89 *Workbook* 5, p.19
Know that condensation occurs when a gas turns into a liquid and that it is the reverse of evaporation.	Unit 5: Changing state • Condensation pp.58–9	*Teacher's Book* 5, pp.74–89 *Workbook* 5, p.19
Know that air contains water vapour and when this meets a cold surface it may condense.	Unit 5: Changing state • Evaporation pp.52–3 • Condensation pp.58–9	*Teacher's Book* 5, pp.74–89
Know that the boiling point of water is 100°C and the melting point of ice is 0°C.	Unit 5: Changing state • Evaporation pp.52–3	*Teacher's Book* 5, pp.74–89
Know that when a liquid evaporates from a solution the solid is left behind.	Unit 5: Changing state • Evaporation pp.52–3	*Teacher's Book* 5, pp.74–89

13

Curriculum structure of *Heinemann Explore Science*

Physics		
Physics: Light		
Observe that shadows are formed when light travelling from a source is blocked.	<u>Unit 4: Light</u> • Blackout blinds pp.40–1 • Changing shadows pp.42–3 • Sunlight and shadows pp.44–5	*Teacher's Book* 5, pp.58–73 *Workbook* 5, p.13
Investigate how the size of a shadow is affected by the position of the object.	<u>Unit 4: Light</u> • Sunlight and shadows pp.44–5	*Teacher's Book* 5, pp.58–73 *Workbook* 5, p.14
Observe that shadows change in length and position throughout the day.	<u>Unit 4: Light</u> • Sunlight and shadows pp.44–5	*Teacher's Book* 5, pp.58–73
Know that light intensity can be measured.	<u>Unit 4: Light</u> • Light sources pp.38–9	*Teacher's Book* 5, pp.58–73
Explore how opaque materials do not let light through and transparent materials let a lot of light through.	<u>Unit 4: Light</u> • Blackout blinds pp.40–1	*Teacher's Book* 5, pp.58–73
Know that we see light sources because light from the source enters our eyes.	<u>Unit 4: Light</u> • Light sources pp.38–9	*Teacher's Book* 5, pp.58–73
Know that beams/rays of light can be reflected by surfaces including mirrors, and when reflected light enters our eyes we see the object.	<u>Unit 4: Light</u> • How we see things pp.46–7	*Teacher's Book* 5, pp.58–73 *Workbook* 5, p.17
Explore why a beam of light changes direction when it is reflected from a surface.	<u>Unit 4: Light</u> • How we see things pp.46–7	*Teacher's Book* 5, pp.58–73 *Workbook* 5, p.16
Physics: The Earth and beyond		
Explore, through modelling, that the sun does not move; its *apparent* movement is caused by the Earth spinning on its axis.	<u>Unit 6: The Earth and beyond</u> • Our turning Earth pp.70–1	*Teacher's Book* 5, pp.90–107
Know that the Earth spins on its axis once in every 24 hours.	<u>Unit 6: The Earth and beyond</u> • Night and day pp.74–5	*Teacher's Book* 5, pp.90–107 *Workbook* 5, p.23,24
Know that the Earth takes a year to orbit the sun, spinning as it goes.	<u>Unit 6: The Earth and beyond</u> • The passing year pp.78–9	*Teacher's Book* 5, pp.90–107
Research the lives and discoveries of scientists who explored the solar system and stars.	<u>Unit 6: The Earth and beyond</u> • Astronomers pp.72–3	*Teacher's Book* 5, pp.90–107

Resources for *Heinemann Explore Science* Grade 5

Science equipment and durable items

angle-poise lamp
bright torch
computer with light sensor
    attachment
digital camera or a video camera
digital microscope
globe
hair dryer
hand fan
hand lenses
hand sprayer for cleaning plant
    leaves
lenses (convex and concave)
lids
light sensor
magnifiers
measuring cylinders

measuring stick
meter rules
microscope
mirror
model heart, either one with
    a pumping mechanism or a
    static one
Newton metres
OHP lamp
opaque objects
petri dishes
plastic bags with wire twist ties
plates
protractors
reflective surface object (not just
    mirrors)
rounders base

rubber tubing (3 different
    thicknesses and sizes)
scalpel (only for use by the
    teacher)
screen
selection of secondary sources,
    books and e-books
sharp knife (only for use by the
    teacher)
small pots
stopwatches
thermometers or temperature
    sensors, connected to a
    computer
timer
torch
white card screen

Consumables and items locally available

antibacterial soap
balloon pump
balloons
balls and spheres
bicycle pump
Blu-tack or sticky tape
bread
card
chalk
clear sandwich bags
clothes pegs
containers
cotton wool
crushed ice
cut-out rocket
empty cigarette packets (to show
    warnings)
empty pill bottles (to show
    warnings)

fast growing seeds, e.g. radish,
    cress, lettuce
food group examples
glass bottles and jars
identical pieces of fabric
kitchen surface cleaner
large simple flowers
leaflets and information
    about drugs and
    medicines
leaflets from fast-food outlets
    (containing detailed dietary
    information)
mugs
paper
ping pong balls
saucers
scissors
seeds for germinating.

several identical pieces of damp
    fabric
shade cards (a strip of paper
    printed in blocks of different
    shades of grey through to
    black)
sticky tape
sugar
tapes
tennis balls
ties for bags
transparent plastic bags or
    containers
trays lined with cotton wool
washing line
washing lines
washing-up bottles
yeast

Unit 1: Microbes

The objectives for this Unit are that students should be able to:

- Understand that all living organisms grow and reproduce

- Know that there are microbes all around people, even inside their bodies, and that people can't live without them

- Learn that microbes or bacteria can be useful or harmful

- Investigate the conditions under which microbes spread.

SB p.1 — Science background

The term microbe or micro-organism describes any living thing too small to be seen with the naked eye. Microbes are all around us. Examples include viruses that cause colds, bacteria that cause sore throats, the 'mould' of penicillin that kills bacteria and the yeast that makes bread rise. Bacteria are among the smallest living things that can exist independently.

At this level, the students will not have to learn the structure of cells, bacteria or viruses, but only be aware of the different names for microbes. Bacteria reproduce asexually, i.e. without the need for both sexes. They divide into two and in the right conditions can do this very quickly. The result of this rapid division is effects we can see, for example colonies of mould on bread or jam.

Freezing, canning, salting and drying all deprive microbes of the conditions to live, grow and reproduce, but microbes are remarkably adaptable. Milk can 'go off' in the fridge close to freezing point. Even frozen food decays over time.

There are both useful and harmful bacteria. Some bacteria are called saprophytes. These live on dead animals and plants, turning them into compost. Some bacteria are parasites. These live on animals and plants that are alive. Some of these cause disease.

Vaccination works by introducing a mild strain of a disease, which makes the blood produce the appropriate white blood cells to kill the invaders. When vaccinated people come into contact with the disease they are able to fight the infection.

Students are not expected to know this much detail in Grade 5, but if some students are curious, this provides a simple explanation. This short Unit requires great emphasis on health and safety.

Language

Bacterium	A small microbe. Some bacteria cause infections, but can be killed by antibiotics, by sterilizing, or by using disinfectants.
Bug	A slang term for a microbe.
Drug	A chemical substance (natural or man-made) that causes a change in our bodies.
Germ	A generic term for a harmful microbe that causes diseases.
Medicine	A drug natural or man-made that causes our body to start to get better or recover from an illness.
Microbe	A living organism too small to be seen with the naked eye, or sometimes even with a microscope. Another word for micro-organism.
Mould	A type of fungus that causes decay.
Pasteurize	A method of preserving food by heating it briefly to a very high temperature to destroy the microbes, leaving the flavour and food value unchanged.
Sterilize	A method of destroying microbes by heating to the boiling point of water.
Virus	A microbe even smaller than a bacterium. They can only become active inside other living cells. They are not affected by antibiotics. Viruses cause flu and colds.
Yeast	One of the largest microbes, a mould used in bread, beer and wine manufacture.

The Words to learn list on page 1 of the *Student Book* can be used to make a classroom display.

Resources

- Microscopes. The digital Intel microscope might not have the magnification to show yeast cells or detail on the mould, but it can show their growth rate.

- Dried or fresh yeast, sugar and balloons.

- Small bottles or similar small vessels with necks that a balloon can fit over.

- Transparent plastic bags with wire twist ties.

- Variety of safe cleaners, e.g. kitchen surface cleaner, antibacterial soap, etc.

- Hand sprayer, e.g. used for cleaning plant leaves, etc. They can be purchased from most garden centres. Make sure it has not been used for pesticides beforehand.

Bright ideas

- If you have a camera that can be attached to a light microscope, this can be set up to show the students some different types of moulds on cheese or other foods.

- Although the Intel microscope doesn't show detail, it can be used to show the rate of mould growth on bread or cheese. Set up the food sample in a container; **Do not** seal it airtight. If using a Petri dish, then put the lid on and place two strips of sticky tape in a cross, to seal the bottom and top loosely together. This ensures students do not remove the lid. Leave the sample under the microscope for several days and set the camera to take pictures every ten minutes to half an hour depending on the warmth of the room.

Knowledge check

Most students will already use the term 'germ' in association with illness, so they may think of all bacteria as harmful. This is not true. They should know that germs are very small.

They should have learned that living things need warmth, food and air to survive. This is true of most microbes as well, though some can exist without air. Students should also be aware of the variety of ways in which foods are preserved to make them last longer. For instance freezing and drying are discussed in the Living and growing Unit in Grade 3.

Skills check

Students need to:

- measure volume and temperature

- make careful observations

- suggest explanations for their investigations using the background science.

Some students will:

- explain how they obtained evidence that yeast is alive

- recognize that some microbes cause food poisoning.

Links to other subjects

Literacy:	Reading and following simple instructions, e.g. setting up the 'Investigating microbes' activity. Writing instructions, e.g. setting out bullet points for the method in 'Investigating microbes'.
Numeracy:	Measuring volume and temperature. Organizing and interpreting simple data in bar graphs or line graphs.
Information Communication Technology (ICT):	Using a digital camera, video or Intel microscope. Using a multimedia package to combine text and graphics to make a presentation.
Personal, Social and Health Education (PSHE):	Learning how to stay well, safe and healthy.

Let's find out ...

The Unit opens with this question:

Do you eat 'fresh food'? You may think you do, but is it really fresh?

Look at the photo. Which of these items are really fresh? Which are preserved? Can you explain why some food is preserved?

17

Unit 1: Microbes – Microbes and you

The objectives for this lesson are that students should be able to:

- Learn how some microbes can be harmful, especially if eaten

- Find out how other microbes help us survive

- Research what microbes can do and related scientific discoveries

- Discover how microbes can be passed from person to person.

SB pp.2–3 | Starter

- Start the lesson by entering the class with a (fake) red nose and an overlarge tissue, blowing your nose and whispering to illustrate that you have a cold. Ask the students what is wrong with you. When they identify that you have a cold, ask them how they think people catch colds, and then introduce the concept of microbes.

- Bring in a mouldy vegetable. *What is happening to this vegetable? Why do you think it is happening? How are vegetables usually preserved to prevent mould? What is mould?*

Explain

Invisible life

Talk briefly about the uses of the words micro-organism and microbe. They mean the same thing but microbe is easier to say and spell. Try to encourage the students to use the scientific terms rather than germ or bug.

Discuss with the students all the illnesses they might have had. Encourage them to suggest illnesses that can be passed from one person to another. People talk about 'catching' a cold, etc.

The yellow fever picture on page 2 of the *Student Book* shows the virus that enters the body and causes the disease. Different diseases are caused by different microbes and they vary in appearance. Illnesses can be diagnosed by taking a blood sample.

Attack!

There are three types of microbe: bacteria, viruses and (some) fungi. Some students may ask about mushrooms. It might amuse them to know that athlete's foot is caused by a type of fungus, or mould, loosely related to mushrooms.

Explain why it is important to dry our feet after washing, brush our teeth regularly and wash our hands after going to the toilet. Link this to using our hands to cover our mouths when we cough or sneeze. This prevents the microbes from spreading to someone else nearby. Many illnesses are caught by touching dirty surfaces and transferring viruses and bacteria to our eyes when we rub them.

Things to do

Making compost

Microbes are essential to life on Earth. Without any microbes at all, we would be left with mountains of waste material that wouldn't decay. We have microbes in our intestines that help us to digest our food.

In the activity, the students set up a small composting heap. This could be done as a whole class, by placing things such as banana skins, apple cores, food packets or newspapers outside, in an area that won't be disturbed. If this is set up on the first session then the items should show some signs of decay by the end of the topic.

> ⚠ The students must not handle rotted material on the compost heap.

Support

Encourage students to predict which things will rot. Remind them that leaves, vegetables, plant materials will rot, as well as paper.

Extend

Some students could predict which items they think will rot first and most from evidence in everyday life. What type of litter is usually left in the streets?

Some students could be given a variety of plastics to see if they rot. Some might be biodegradable.

Record

The students can draw the item before and after rotting. They could take digital pictures of the item before and after or as a time delay to show the process of decay.

I wonder...

The word 'bacterium' is the singular.

Dig deeper

Students have the opportunity to find out more about the scientists who discovered the existence of microbes.

Louis Pasteur, Anton van Leeuwenhoek and Edward Jenner all studied microbes. Having observed the effect of certain microbes, they set about trying to destroy harmful ones with vaccinations, inoculations and pasteurization.

Did you know?

These facts put the size of microbes in context and also underline the destructive power of such small organisms.

- There are over 500 types of cold virus although they all produce similar symptoms. This may be why we can catch colds so often, because so many are unrecognized by our bodies.

Other ideas...

Compost

Develop the compost areas set up by the students so that it can be added to throughout the year. Link compost to the idea of recycling and reducing waste.

Here are the estimated rotting times of some everyday materials:

Orange peel and banana skin: 2 years.

Food packets: 20 years.

Aluminium drink cans: 100 years.

Glass bottles: A million years.

Plastic bottles: Nobody knows. Possibly never.

Compost bins

Investigate the design of compost bins. Why do they have holes in them? Why do you take the compost from the bottom and not the top? Is a plastic container the best type to have?

Presentation

Ask the students to produce a PowerPoint presentation using the time-lapse pictures of their 'Making compost' activity to illustrate the importance of not leaving litter about, especially litter that won't rot. They could also discuss how some of the items could be recycled.

At home

WS 1

Ask the students to produce a chart that shows all the times they do something at home to avoid spreading germs, e.g. washing hands, wiping surfaces, cleaning teeth, etc. They can fill it in as a tally chart and then produce a bar chart of the results for display.

Ask students to complete WS 1.

Plenary

Show some safe cleaners, e.g. anti-bacterial kitchen and bathroom cleaners, antibacterial hand soap, etc. What would happen if we didn't keep our kitchens and bathrooms relatively germ free?

19

Unit 1: Microbes – Investigating microbes

The objectives for this lesson are that students should be able to:

- Find out under what conditions the microbes grow well

- Plan and carry out a scientific investigation to measure the growth of microbes

- Understand that this experiment must be carried out safely as the microbes they are growing can be harmful

- Explain whether the evidence shows that microbes are living things.

SB pp.4–5 | Starter

- This will need setting up previously, but is easy to do. Leave a cheese sandwich and a half eaten apple in a warm place, in a transparent plastic storage tub with the lid on. After about a week, the bread will have started to dry up and there should be some small blue/green mould growths on it.

- Share this with the class and discuss why this has happened. You could make out that you are so hungry you are about to eat your lunch, then 'discover' the mouldy sandwich. Question the students about what they think happened. Act innocent about the conditions you kept it in.

- You could bring in an item of fresh food that has a 'use by' date on it, and discuss what this means and where you should keep the food. Does the food have storage instructions on it already? Pose the 'wondering' question: 'what happens if I don't keep the food as recommended?'

The challenge

Read the opening section of page 4 in the *Student Book*. Ask the students where they think the microbes are being kept. (In the fridge!) What conditions are ideal for them to grow and reproduce?

What to do

The challenge is for the students to find out what conditions the microbes need for rapid growth and reproduction. They also need to decide how to measure the growth, either the rate of growth or the total growth in a set time.

The first suggestion by Class 5J investigates the type of food required by the microbes. Different microbes grow on different foods, so the results will not be conclusive.

The other suggestion is equally valid.

> ⚠️ **Do not** open the plastic bags/ containers once they are closed. The microbes and moulds that grow on bread are relatively safe but when microbes reproduce they produce airborne spores that some people are allergic to. Opening the bags will release the spores. When the investigation is finished, the bread mould grown in the plastic bags **must** be safely disposed of in the bags **without** opening them.
>
> If you have used containers, immerse the container in a dilute bleach or sterilizing solution before opening. Wear disposable gloves and wash the containers thoroughly. Keep bleach and disinfectant locked away.

What you need

- bread

- plastic bags, Petri dishes or similar containers

- ties for the plastic bags

What to check

The bread samples should all be the same size. The plastic bags/containers should allow some gases in and out, so the microbes don't respire anaerobically. The students need to decide if they are going to count the number of colonies at the end of a set time for all the samples, or count the colonies every day. The second option would be suited for the more able, especially if they are designing their table themselves. To make it fair, the students will need to measure the amount of water put on the surface of the bread.

> ⚠️ Students will need to wash their hands after setting up the investigation.

Support

The students should not eat any of the bread. Not only does it alter the amount of bread, making the investigation unfair, but they should be taught that it is bad practice to eat in science lessons.

Extend

The students could design their own table to record the number of colonies on the board every day. Students should also consider how the fridge light might affect the growth of the mould. In reality, not much, but it depends how often they open the door to check!

Can you do better? WS 2

Show the students Class 5J's report on WS 2. Read it together.

The investigation is very simple, and the students in Class 5J have written their instructions, or method, clearly. However, Class 5J don't give any reasons for their prediction. They could have suggested that if a microbe was a living thing it would have the same requirements to grow well as other living organisms. Students should also suggest that to obtain really reliable results it is necessary to repeat the observations several times.

What did you find? WS 3

The students could draw their own table or use the table on WS 3.

Record

The students could convert their recorded data into a graph. If necessary, they could use Class 5J's data given in the *Student Book*. A bar chart can be produced of this data to show which bread sample had the most number of growths on it.

Present

Students should present their ideas to the rest of the class. At the same time as leaving the bread in different places, one could be placed in a Petri dish as described before, under a digital recording microscope with time lapse, such as an Intel microscope, Easi-Scope or ViTiny USB microscope. The camera can be set to take pictures every hour so the decaying process of the bread can be run like a film.

Now predict

Your students should be able to tell Class 5A that they need to keep their food in a cold and dry environment. This could be in the form of a set of package instructions or an instruction sheet for Class 5A.

Other ideas...

Mushrooms

Although mushrooms aren't microbes, they do have smaller fungal relatives. You could grow mushrooms from a kit. Usually they start growing in the dark. Ask the students to think why. The hyphae are underground and the mushroom is the fruiting body. It produces millions of spores.

ICT ideas
Graphing

All the data from each of the students' investigations could be entered into a graphing program to produce a graph of class results.

Video

The video could be set to film the mushrooms growing. As the students can see them actually growing they are more likely to believe that they are alive.

At home WS 4

Ask the students to look at the different wrappings used for bread and to look at the way it is sealed. Is it airtight? Why does the packaging have dates written on it?

Ask students to complete WS 4.

Plenary

The students will need to have tried to explain why the microbes require warmth and water to grow well. What other things have these requirements? Which part of the investigation showed that these microbes were not plants? (They had no need for light.)

Unit 1: Microbes – Using microbes

The objectives for this lesson are that students should be able to:

- Discover how microbes can be used to make food or drink

- Find out that microbes can cause people to be ill

- Understand that microbes can be used in medication to kill the bugs making people ill

- Investigate how yeast is made and how it produces carbon dioxide gas.

SB pp.6–7

Starter

- Have a quick-fire word association game. You give the students a word and they tell you what it reminds them of. Use words like germ, chickenpox, sneeze, mould, etc. Write a list on the board. If the students decide to write down the word then be sure they tell you their first thoughts, not what they come up with after several minutes.

- Show a picture of bread (or some real bread). *What other foods can you name that use microbes in their manufacture?* Cheese, yoghurt and tofu are good examples.

Explain

Edible mould

Show some mould-produced foods. In promoting the plus points about microbes, point out that they are essential to making leavened bread, cheese, yoghurt, vinegar, yeast extract or Marmite and many high-protein meat substitutes. They are essential to the production of many medicines, and the breakdown of sewage.

Reiterate some of the rules that the students may have learned in food technology lessons about where to store objects in the fridge and which colour chopping boards restaurants use for particular foods. Raw meat goes at the bottom of the fridge, so that any blood doesn't drip on the foods below. Cooked meats go higher up the fridge. The vegetables go in the 'crisper' at the bottom. When chopping food, restaurants use a red board for raw meat and a green one for vegetables and salads.

Microbe wars

Biotechnology is a fast growing area of industry. With advances made in making new drugs to cure illness, some diseases have been virtually eradicated, including smallpox and polio. Methods of detecting diseases have improved so that they can be caught at an earlier stage and treated effectively.

Things to do

How yeast rises

Once you set up a yeast culture, the students should see some bubbles forming, like a froth. Put the yeast, with some sugar, in different temperatures of water, in small bottles loosely stoppered with cotton wool. Alternatively, a balloon can be put over the neck of the bottle. The carbon dioxide gas produced by the yeast will cause the balloon to inflate. The hotter the water used, the faster the yeast grows and the more gas it produces, so the bigger the balloon. If water that is too hot is used, this kills the yeast. Heat kills microbes. They are not killed by cold but become dormant. Food kept in a freezer is still susceptible to decay.

Dried yeast from a supermarket can be used for this activity, but it will take about 30 minutes to work. Live yeast may be available. Leaving a mixture of flour and water (the consistency of thick cream or batter) in a warm place and mixing daily for about a week will produce a natural yeast. The quantities are not critical, as the yeast will continue to grow until it kills itself with its own waste products.

Support

Show students how to stretch the balloons before they fit them on to the bottle necks, and blow the balloons up once beforehand, as this stretches the rubber.

Extend

Most students will know that carbon dioxide gas is being produced by the yeast. Some students will be able to relate the production of this gas to respiration, especially if they have been told its name. This suggests the yeast is alive.

Some students could measure the circumference of the balloons and find the optimum temperature for the yeast. Use water at different temperatures, keeping all other variables the same, i.e. amount of water, sugar and yeast.

Record

If the students measured the balloon circumference, this can be presented as a table of results and perhaps a line graph. If some of the water was too hot and the yeast died, this will be apparent on the graph. The students could draw a diagram of what they did and record their observations, explaining why they think yeast is alive.

I wonder...

Freezing deprives the microbes of warmth. They aren't killed but it is too cold for them to breed. They will start to reproduce again when warm.

Drying deprives microbes of water.

Curing, salting and jam-making all draw water out of the microbes. The dehydrated microbes cannot grow and reproduce.

Subjecting food to a dose of radiation isn't harmful to the food, but kills microbes.

Dig deeper

Students have the opportunity to find out about the scientist Alexander Fleming.

Did you know?

These facts tell students of the different ways of preserving food and also that biotechnology is a fast-growing industry.

Other ideas...

WS 5

Bread making

If you have hygienic cooking conditions, you could investigate dough types or dough rising conditions using WS 5. You could make unleavened bread without yeast and compare the texture with leavened bread.

Bread tins

This is related to the above activity. Set students a design and technology task to design the best-shaped bread tin. They will need to keep in mind how the bread will change while baking and what shape the finished product should be. The sides of the tin need to be taller than a cake tin, or the rising bread will flow over the top.

Presentation

The students could video their bread rising and use it as part of a presentation to the rest of the class about the use of yeast in bread making, taking care to mention that yeast is a living organism.

The students could do a presentation to show how aware they are of basic food hygiene. They could draw a fridge and label where to place all their weekly shopping. This can be assembled into a large display on the wall, perhaps as a kitchen with the food preparation areas marked on it.

At home

Ask the students to make a table of all the foods they eat over one week and how they are preserved. They could then produce a graph of the results to see what type of preservation is most common.

Plenary

WS 6

The students could write a short rhyme to help them remember the basic hygiene rules in the kitchen, or how diseases are spread. Alternatively, they could fill in WS 6.

Unit 1: Microbes – Unit 1: Review

The objectives for this lesson are that students should be able to:

- Check what they have learned about microbes in this Unit

- Find out how they are working towards, within and beyond the Grade 5 level.

SB p.8

Expectations

Students working towards Grade 5 level will:

- Recognize that very small living things can cause illness.

- Begin to link their evidence with their knowledge and understanding.

In addition, students working within Grade 5 level will:

- Recognize that there are many very small organisms which can cause illness or decay.

- Recognize that microbes can be used in food production.

- Recognize that these microbes feed, grow and reproduce like other organisms.

- Microbes can be both harmful and helpful.

- Decay can be both useful and harmful.

- Humans produce treatments for illnesses using microbes.

- Make relevant observations and draw conclusions from them.

- Suggest explanations for their conclusions using their scientific knowledge and understanding.

Further to this, students working beyond Grade 5 level will also:

- Describe evidence that yeast is living.

- Explain how microbes can move from one food source to another and how this can cause food poisoning.

- Explain how their evidence supports their conclusion.

Check-up

Discuss why we have to wash our hands before meals, especially if we have been working with animals or soil.

The students will still have microbes on their hands that were in the soil or on the animals they were examining. These can be transferred to their food and then ingested. There, they have a warm and moist place to breed. They might then cause a stomach upset, similar to food poisoning.

Assessment

WS 7

Use the Unit 1 assessment on WS 7 to check the students' understanding of the content of the Unit. The answers are given opposite.

Name: _____ Date: _____

WS 7

Unit 1 assessment

1 Complete the table. Show whether each of these microbes is helpful or harmful.

Microbe	Helpful	Harmful
mould on bread		
bacteria in yoghurt		
yeast in bread		
mould in cheese		
bacteria in compost		
virus for 'flu		

2 Some scientists wanted to see if washing hands prevented the spread of microbes. They tested their theory with bread. They set up the experiment in sealed bags and left it for 5 days. These are their results.

Conditions of bread	Number of colonies
clean hand wiped over surface of bread	5
freshly washed hand wiped over surface of bread	1
dirty hand wiped over surface of bread	10
bread wiped across surface of the floor	15

a) Draw a bar chart of these results on a sheet of paper.

b) How does washing your hands prevent microbes from spreading?

_____

_____

Unit 1: Microbes   7

Answers

Unit 1 assessment

1

Microbe	Helpful?	Harmful?
Mould on bread		✓
Bacteria in yoghurt	✓	
Yeast in bread	✓	
Mould in cheese	✓	
Bacteria in compost	✓	
Virus for 'flu		✓

2　a　The bar chart should be labelled with a title on both axes. The x-axis should be the 'conditions' the bread had and the y-axis labelled with 'number of colonies'.

b　Washing prevents microbes spreading.

⚠ Never grow microbes from dirty hands in the classroom. You will have no control over what grows.

The answer!

Refer back to the introductory question.

Of the food shown in the picture on page 1 of the *Student Book*, the oranges may be fresh but may have been kept in the fridge with the milk and butter. The tea was dried before it was used. Jam is called a preserve, because you cook the fruit with sugar to preserve it, then seal it in jars, similar to canning. Without yeast the bread wouldn't rise.

And finally...

The students could find out about some of the cleaners used to eliminate microbes, deciding what microbes they are targeted at. This could be used to produce a large display of the areas in a kitchen that harbour microbes and the ways in which they can be eliminated.

25

Unit 2: Keeping healthy

The objectives for this Unit are that students should be able to:

- Understand that animals, including humans, need a variety of foods to survive

- Investigate the benefits of exercise on their bodies

- Learn that some drugs, such as tobacco, can harm their bodies, whereas others, such as medicine, can help them

- Explain what the heart does and why people should keep their hearts healthy.

SB p.9   Science background

This Unit builds on Living and growing in Grade 3 and Humans and animals in Grade 4. Students need to know that some foods provide energy, either immediate or stored (carbohydrates and fats). Some students will know that carbohydrates come in different forms including sugar and starch. Protein foods are necessary for growth; fresh fruit and vegetables are needed for general health and also provide fibre.

When doing the exercise activity, the students should only undertake normal PE-type activities and not push themselves too hard or fast to see what their pulse rate becomes. A child's pulse is about 80–90 beats per minute, at rest. This decreases with age to about 65 beats per minute.

The topic informs students of the need to take regular exercise and to avoid misuse or abuse of medicines and drugs. Their parents may use cigarettes or indeed other drugs, and you will need to be sensitive about this issue. The word 'drug' has illegal connotations, but all substances that affect our bodies, our mood or our behaviour are drugs. Medicines are drugs that are taken to promote health or to combat disease. All medicines are drugs, but not all drugs are medicines. A drug is any substance that has an effect on our body, good or bad. A medicine has a beneficial effect; but even medicines can be misused or abused.

Language

Artery	Thick-walled blood vessel that carries blood away from the heart: oxygenated blood to the body; deoxygenated blood to the lungs.
Balanced diet	A diet that contains a healthy mix of protein, fibre, fat, carbohydrate and vitamins and minerals.
Capillary	Fine, thin-walled blood vessel that connects arteries and veins. Substances can pass through capillary walls.
Carbohydrate	Provides the body with energy. Found in foods such as bread, rice, pasta, potatoes and sugar.
Pulse	Pressure wave pushed through the body by the heart. You can feel a pulse where blood vessels are near the surface of the body.
Side effect	Any feeling after taking a drug; often unwanted.
Starch	Food group produced by plants as a food store that provides immediate energy.
Sugar	Food group that provides immediate energy.
Vein	Thin-walled blood vessel that carries blood towards the heart: deoxygenated blood from the body; oxygenated blood from the lungs.
Vessel	A hollow tube with varying thickness of walls that carries blood around the body.

The Words to learn list on page 9 of the *Student Book* can be used to make a classroom display.

Resources

- *Keeping Healthy* Reader.

- Examples of all the food groups. These can either be pictures, packets or actual foods. Use them to recap the food groups.

- Stopwatches.

- Leaflets from fast-food outlets. They may contain detailed dietary information, telling you how much fat, sugar, starch, energy, etc. is in each product.

- A bicycle pump or balloon pump and some balloons.

- Empty washing-up bottles.

- A model heart, either one with a pumping mechanism or a static one.

- Leaflets and information about drugs and medicines.

- Empty pill bottles and cigarette packets to show the warnings on them and information about dosage.

- Rubber tubing in at least three different thicknesses and sizes.

Bright ideas

- If you have a digital pulse meter or a heart monitor, use it to check the accuracy of the students' readings.

- A microphone and tape recorder can be useful in the enquiry.

- An old washing-up bottle that is fairly flexible and can be squeezed in 'pulses' is a good way to demonstrate the heart squeezing its muscles to push blood out and around the body. Students can see the force with which it leaves the heart. If you then attach a piece of rubber tubing, the students should be able to feel the 'pulse' as they rest their fingers lightly on the tube while you squeeze the bottle. Compare this to pressing their blood vessels onto a bone to feel their pulse.

- Invite a drugs education visitor or an appropriate police officer to talk about drugs. This is one way of raising the students' awareness of illegal drugs. Refer to your school policy.

Knowledge check

- Students should be able to name body parts.

- Students should recognize common food types.

- Students should understand that we need to eat to grow and be healthy.

- Students should understand that to be healthy they need a balanced diet.

Skills check

Students need to:

- repeat measurement charts

- represent data in bar charts and graphs and interpret them

- use their results to draw conclusions.

Some students will:

- explain why they need to repeat their measurements on pulse rate

- explain why they should test several people's pulses.

Links to other subjects

Literacy: Reading and following simple instructions, e.g. squeezing the bottle 'heart'.

Numeracy: Organizing and interpreting simple data in tables – e.g. pulse rate against exercise time.

Multiplying, e.g. calculating the beats per minute by timing the pulse for 15 seconds and multiplying by 4.

ICT: Using a digital pulse meter or heart monitor. Using PowerPoint to produce a presentation.

PSHE: Developing a healthy, safe lifestyle, including healthy eating and exercise as well as looking at the purpose of medicines and drugs.

Let's find out ...

The Unit opens with this question:

If an adult was lazy, overweight and smoked, why might their doctor worry about their health? What might the doctor suggest they do? What kind of food would the doctor suggest they eat? What other things might they do to stay healthy?

Discuss the problem. Students may not realize that a lot of exercise without preparation and build-up can do a lot of damage. Discuss the different types of exercise that could be taken. Point out that everyone can be fit – but that fitness for an elderly person is different from fitness for a rugby player.

Unit 2: Keeping healthy – Keeping fit

The objectives for this lesson are that students should be able to:

- Find out what makes a healthy, balanced diet

- Discover what else people need to stay healthy

- Make a list and/or chart of how much fruit and vegetables they eat

- Understand how our muscles work when we exercise.

SB pp.10–11 — Starter

- Show a picture of a beautiful well-presented meal from a magazine or recipe book, or use a real meal. Be sensitive to cultural food differences. If you use a real meal, ensure it contains foods that the students would want to eat. Also take in an equivalent meal that is messy and unappealing, maybe burnt or overcooked. *Which one would you like to eat? Why?* Explain that both are balanced meals. Remind the students of the different food groups and what they provide us with.

- Bring in your 'lunch box'. In it, have chocolate, crisps, carrot sticks, hummus and a can of fizzy drink. Ask students whether your lunch is healthy or not. How can they tell?

Explain

Chocolate ice cream and fries

If chocolate ice cream and fries sounds bizarre, ask the students to come up with their favourite meal. If they had this every day, even if it is balanced, for example, chicken, potatoes and vegetables, they would soon be fed up as it would become boring. A diet should be varied, not only to make sure it is balanced, but interesting enough to make us want to eat the food too. When you serve up a meal, presentation and taste are both important.

How much energy do you need?

Kilocalories (kcal) are an imperial measure for energy; some students will probably recognize that their parents count calories. They are also the main energy value quoted on the nutritional part of packets. Kilojoules (kJ) are metric units for energy.

Remind the students of what happens when they exercise, i.e. they feel hot and tired as their muscles work harder. The energy in their food provides them with the energy to exercise as well as to live. Even when they are asleep, their bodies, including heart muscles and brain, still need energy to keep them alive.

Things to do — WS 8

Apples, oranges, peas, carrots and peppers!

Fresh fruit and vegetables provide vitamins and minerals as well as fibre to our diet. The activity can be done retrospectively if you want to get an instant picture, i.e. ask the students what they ate in previous days, although some students will be unable to remember what they ate yesterday.

Record

When writing the foods as a list, the students can turn this into a table similar to the one on WS 8. Let them turn the data into a bar chart of food types and number of pieces. A different colour could be used for each day. Alternatively, make a bar chart of days of the week and pieces of food.

Support

Use WS 8 to help students make the original list or turn it into a table. They can fill in some fruit and vegetables they have eaten as well as using the ones already in the table.

Extend

Most students will be able to record the number of pieces of fruit or vegetables they eat each day. Some should be able to turn their data into a pie chart to show which fruit or vegetable they ate most of in the week and tell the 'story' of their chart.

I wonder...

Rice and pasta are foods which contain starch for immediate energy. Fresh fruit and vegetables provide the vitamins and minerals that will keep an athlete healthy, but fruit contains sugar too. Lots of athletes eat a good helping of bananas for immediate energy; ripe bananas are easy to digest.

Dig deeper

The students have an opportunity to further their knowledge of what they should do to be fit and healthy, including getting plenty of sleep.

Did you know?

Facts here will remind students that they need energy from food to grow and be active.

The average human body contains enough fat to make seven bars of soap!

Women burn fat more slowly than men by a rate of 50 calories per day, so women, on average, need less energy intake from food than men.

Other ideas

A healthy burger meal?

Use the nutritional information from fast-food outlets to see if they can provide a balanced meal, including all four food groups. Work on the basis that the meal should be about one-third of the students' calorie intake for the day.

A three-day walk

Ask the students to produce a set of meals that a walker would use. Explain that as they have to carry all their food, it has got to be lightweight. Students will need to think about the weight and bulk of the food and the energy values they have.

Eating sensibly

Set the students a design and technology task to design a food label. The label should clearly show the food group the product falls into and other ingredients and could have pictures to illustrate the contents.

Presentation

Ask the students to pretend they are designers for a large food manufacturing company or a fast-food outlet. They should present their student-friendly food labels, explaining why their new labels should be put on the food product.

Ask the students to create an advert to sell their favourite food to each other. These could be filmed to display during an open evening, or the students could use photographs of the product to create a wall display showing the features they want to emphasize.

At home

Ask students to look at the nutritional information on some food packets. Which food that you ate this week contains the most energy? What would happen if you ate lots of it and didn't exercise? Ask them to compare products that are the same but have a 'light' option. What differences are there in the energy values?

Plenary

Show students an example of a menu from a restaurant. Let them produce one of their own that shows, in an interesting way, all the healthy foods they should eat. Let them design it on a computer. They should include an attractive name for the meals, as well as a description of what they contain. They should also include the food types and how each one is beneficial.

Discuss with the students why they need to eat and which parts of their body need the most energy when they are exercising. Ask them to explain which foods they should eat to ensure they have plenty of energy to exercise.

New International Edition

Unit 2: Keeping healthy – Your heart

The objectives for this lesson are that students should be able to:

- Explain how their heart is protected by their ribs

- Understand how the heart pumps blood around their bodies

- Make a washing-up bottle pump to demonstrate how the heart works

- Research more about the heart in both humans and other animals.

SB pp.12–13 — Starter

Show a picture of a skeleton. Use it to support your teaching in these activities.

Review the structure of the skeleton and its function to remind students that it is for protection as well as movement and support. Play a game to remind students of the names of the bones. Discuss the main function of the skull and ribs, i.e. protection of the brain and heart and lungs, respectively.

Enter the classroom wearing as many items of protection as you can, e.g. goggles, helmet, shin pads, shoulder pads, gloves, steel-toed boots, cricket pads, etc. *Why have I got all this on?* After a discussion on protection, remove any items that cover the bony parts of your body, e.g. ribs, head. Say that they are still protected, but ask what by.

Explain

Crash hats and ribcages

Crash hats, of course, protect our brains. Shin pads protect our shins! It's not that our shins are as important as our brains, but that they are the part of our body most likely to get hurt during a game, such as football. We protect parts of our body either because they have a very important function, or because they are likely to get hurt.

Can your heart speak?

By placing your hands over your ears quite tightly and sitting quietly for a few seconds you can hear your heart. In fact, you are hearing a pulse in your head as you are pushing on an artery. The normal sound is 'lub-dub' or similar. A doctor can tell there is a problem if the sound changes.

Things to do

Your very own pump

Perform this activity outside and take care to ensure that no one gets wet! Also make sure that the washing-up bottles have been cleaned so that if water is flying about there won't be any soap in it.

Record

Students can draw a bar chart of their results and determine, from the height of the squeezed water, who had the strongest squeeze.

Support

Help the students to measure the height of the water. One way of doing this is to squirt the water up a brick wall and work out the height afterwards. Measuring in courses of bricks will eliminate actually having to measure the height.

Extend

All students should recognize that the harder you squeeze the bottle the further the water shoots. Most will relate this to how hard the heart must squeeze to pump the blood.

Some students may be able to say what else they need to ensure the water in the bottle reaches 10 m, i.e. a sudden sharp squeeze.

I wonder...

You can find a pulse wherever a blood vessel is close to the skin – usually at joints in the body such as the wrist.

Dig deeper

Students have the opportunity to find out more about the heart and its valves. Valves prevent the blood from flowing backwards. They are flaps of tissue which operate like swing doors – they open one way, but can't be pushed the other way. If the valves in your heart or main vessels don't work properly they can be replaced with artificial ones.

Did you know?

These facts illustrate that the heart is an important organ.

The heart beats about 100 000 times per day and pumps a total of 36 000 l (8000 gallons) of blood about 19 000 km (12 000 miles) around the body every day.

Other ideas

Listening device

Set the students a design technology task of making a stethoscope to listen to their heart. Rubber tubing and small plastic funnels will do the job.

They will need to join two pieces of tubing together if they want to listen in stereo, e.g. by means of a T-piece. Old-fashioned listening devices were made of a single large 'trumpet'; the students could try to make one of these instead using card or paper. *What shape is best?* The stethoscope conducts sound directly to the ear. It was also successful at cutting out extraneous sound.

Working harder

Ask the students to clench and unclench their fists for one minute while their arms are by their sides. Then repeat the exercise with their hands over their heads. The students should feel more tired and find it harder to do the second exercise. Discuss how hard the heart must be working to pump the blood up the arms, rather than down them.

Presentation

Ask the students to pretend to be experts on listening devices and to give a lecture on which shape is best for a listening device. They could use PowerPoint as part of the presentation, using any research findings about the development of stethoscopes.

Display the listening devices that the students have made. Research on the Internet may reveal some more information and images to add to the display.

At home

Ask students to use secondary sources to find out where the heart is found in different animals. They should find that the heart is always protected by the ribs.

Plenary

Ask the students to describe what the muscles of the heart must be like to be able to pump the blood so far. How do the rest of your muscles feel when they work that hard? Ask the students to write a poem to describe what their heart sounds like and how the sound changes when they exercise.

Unit 2: Keeping healthy – Pumping blood

The objectives for this lesson are that students should be able to:

- Find out how blood gets carried around their bodies

- Tell the difference between the three different types of blood vessels

- Learn what blood carries around their bodies

- Make a labelled diagram of the heart's chambers and vessels.

SB pp.14–15 | Starter

Show a video (or a diagram) of the heart pumping the blood to remind the students that the lower chambers of the heart (the ventricles) squeeze the blood out and so have thicker muscular walls than the atria. The left side has more muscle as it has to pump the blood all the way round the body.

If you have a static model of the heart, use it to show the size and the actual shape of the heart.

Explain

Three for one

The three types of blood vessel are arteries, capillaries and veins. The arteries always carry blood away from the heart. They carry blood rich in oxygen to the body. They have thick walls so that they don't burst under the pressure of the heart pumping the blood. Capillaries have very thin walls, only one cell thick, and are only big enough to allow red blood cells to travel down them in single file. This allows the oxygen to be dropped off to the muscles. The veins carry de-oxygenated blood back towards the heart from the body. The artery going from the heart to the lung carries blood depleted of oxygen as it goes to the lungs to pick it up. The vein, which goes from the lung back to the heart, carries the blood rich in oxygen.

Blood's journey

This is a short, story-style piece to illustrate how the blood moves around the circulatory system. The picture illustrates where the organs are by the collection of blood vessels in certain areas. The two different colours represent red arteries and blue veins. In reality, blood is not so clearly different in colour and the colour of the veins (in the wrist, for example) is due to seeing them through tissues rather than a lack of oxygen. Capillaries are too numerous and small to be shown.

Things to do | WS 9

How does it work?

Initially the students will need some help remembering which side of the heart is the left, as this seems wrong at first. The left side is our left as the heart is in our body, as if we were looking down on it in our chests, rather than looking at it as if we were facing it. The diagram will need to be labelled carefully.

The word atrium comes from the Latin for 'central court' and the word ventricle comes from the Latin word venter for 'belly' or 'womb'. So, the atrium is the hallway and the ventricle is the main body of the heart.

Record

By labelling the diagram of the heart on WS 9, students will have a record from which to learn the names of its parts.

Support

Ask the students to put their diagram of the heart on their chests and look down at it. This will help them to see better which side is left and which is right.

Extend

Most students should be able to label the four chambers of the heart as ventricles and atria. Some may be able to label the main artery as the aorta and the main vein as the vena cava, and the vessels that link the heart to the lungs as pulmonary artery and pulmonary vein, but this is not essential at this stage.

I wonder...

The heart is an involuntary muscle as it works without instruction from the brain. A muscle that needs a signal from the brain to operate is called voluntary muscle. We have no direct control over our heart rate, but it changes in response to body activity.

Dig deeper

Students have the opportunity to find out more about the heart and its role in supplying oxygenated blood to our cells. We need blood to go to every one of our cells as they need oxygen to survive.

Did you know?

These facts relate to the amount of work that the heart does in its lifetime.

Ancient Egyptians thought the heart was the centre of intelligence and emotion. They thought the brain was not significant, so removed it through the nose during mummification and discarded it!

Other ideas

WS 10

How the heart works

WS 10 will allow students to label the parts of the heart and to explain the process of the blood moving through the body.

Presentation

Let the students work in groups to use ICT to present information about the transport system in their body. They can show how the heart beats and pumps the blood around the body.

At home

Ask the students to write a short story of the blood as it moves through the heart. Alternatively, they could continue the extract used in the *Student Book*.

Plenary

Discuss why we need a heart and blood in our bodies. Do other animals have a heart and blood? Go through the differences between the types of blood vessel. Show some rubber tubing of different thicknesses, e.g. drainage pipe, a garden hose and some micro-tubing. Which blood vessels do these represent? If you only have two types, ask which one is missing. What would it look like?

New International Edition

Unit 2: Keeping healthy – Counting heartbeats

The objectives for this lesson are that students should be able to:

- Understand the effect exercise has on their heart rate

- Learn how to measure their heart rate

- Find and record all the places on their body they can feel their pulse

- Determine the average pulse rate for the class and present their findings.

SB pp.16–17

Starter

- Ask the students to find their heartbeat. Then ask them to place one hand over their heart and one on a pulse point. Are they both the same?

- Enter the classroom as if you have been running. Breathe heavily. *Why do I have to breathe so quickly?* Most students will know that there is less oxygen, and more carbon dioxide, in the air you breathe out. They should be able to link a higher breathing rate with more activity. *What do you think my heart is doing? Why?*

Explain

Faster, faster

The heart pumps the blood around the body to deliver oxygen to all the cells of the body. At the same time it delivers dissolved food. The blood then picks up waste products of carbon dioxide and water as well as waste such as urea. The carbon dioxide is removed from the body as we breathe. The urea and other waste products are removed by the kidneys.

Give it a rest

The heart has mini rests so that it has no need to stop beating during our lives. The rest is approximately less than a quarter of a second. As this happens at every beat, it adds up to a lot of time – hence the heart rests for almost 40 years during its 70 years of work. This is a similar analogy to the one that says we spend one-third of our life asleep (based on eight hours sleep a night).

Things to do

How fast is yours?

Many students will have difficulty in finding their pulse. Some find their pulse most easily on their temple. If you push too hard on the pulse you can't feel it, so check the students are only pressing lightly. The reason for using the fingers rather than the thumb for this activity is that the thumb has its own pulse.

Record

Once all the students have checked their pulse rate and are sure they have an accurate reading, let them add it to a class table. Each student can then produce a bar chart of the class's pulse rates. They should be able to recognize that their pulse rates are all similar when at rest.

Support

Some student may lose count of their pulse rate. Ask them to work in pairs and count out aloud so their partner can monitor their counting.

Extend

Most students should be able to count their pulse over one minute but realize that they need to take it several times to be sure they have an accurate reading.

Some students may be able to take their pulse for 15 seconds and multiply the result by four, then check if the same number of beats per minute are recorded.

I wonder...

The larger the animal the slower its heart rate will be.

Dig deeper

Students have the opportunity to find out more about blood pressure. Blood pressure is the force with which the heart pushes the blood around the body. Doctors and nurses use this as one measure of general health. When we are unwell our blood pressure may change. If we have a fright our heart will speed up and blood pressure will increase.

Did you know?

These facts show students that the hearts of different animals beat at different rates.

Other ideas

WS 11

Find your pulse

Part of the 'I wonder' in the previous lesson was to find as many places as possible to feel your heartbeat. Ask the students to show you some of these. The main places will be the wrist (about 4 cm below the ball of the thumb), the neck (just at the end of the jaw, underneath the ear) and the groin. Your pulse can also be detectable underneath the armpit.

Ask students to complete WS 11 marking the places where they found their pulse.

Circulation game

Ask the students to produce a board game that shows how blood is transported round the body and what it does at each station, e.g. lungs – collect oxygen and drop off carbon dioxide, stomach – drop off oxygen and pick up waste, etc. The game could have either a spinner or a dice to get around the board. Suggest that they have to collect tokens to build up a picture of the circulatory system.

Presentation

Encourage the students to pretend that they are teachers. They have to explain what the average pulse rate is for their class. Point out that they will need to explain what the pulse rate is first.

Ask the students to create and display a large outline of the body to show where their heart is and all the pulse points they can find.

The students could do a large scale table and graph of the class's results from the activity measuring pulse rates at rest.

At home

WS 12

Refer students to WS 12. Ask them to take heart rates of as many people at rest and of different ages as possible at home. Tell them to make sure that the readings are accurate. They will need to repeat the count three times for each reading to check. What pattern do they notice?

Encourage some students to draw a line graph of people's age against their pulse rate.

Plenary

Using the graph, discuss which was the most commonly recorded pulse rate and who had the lowest and highest. Ask why the range of pulse rates is quite small, i.e. because all the students were resting. Ask the students why they needed to take their pulse more than once. Discuss where you might get an error. More able students, who have compared taking the pulse for one minute and then for 15 seconds and multiplying by four, could comment on the accuracy of their method.

Unit 2: Keeping healthy – Investigating pulse rate

The objectives for this lesson are that students should be able to:

- Find out what affects their pulse rate

- Decide what measurements to take

- Develop methods of making their experiment fair

- Evaluate their own and Class 5E's results.

SB pp.18–19 — Starter

- Show a picture of an artificial heart and discuss what its purpose might be. Although it looks like an old fashioned diving helmet, you can see the valves where the blood goes in and out of the heart. It is driven by compressed air to make it pump. *What happens when you exercise?* Pump a bicycle pump hard and fast to demonstrate this. You could also show this with a squeezy bottle and some rubber tubing, as described earlier.

The challenge

Read the What to do and conversation on page 18 in the *Student Book*. Discuss the different ways the groups in Class 5E decided to carry out the experiment and collect their evidence.

At this stage, students should be aware of the need to check their evidence to see how reliable it is. Taking the pulse once will not be reliable. So the first suggestion will not give an accurate set of results.

The second suggestion is much better as the evidence is being checked by taking the pulse three times. If the activity is changing, the data will not be continuous so the students will be able to produce a bar chart of their results.

The third suggestion will produce reliable data and a line graph as the data will be continuous. The longer you exercise for, the higher your pulse rate will rise. Eventually, it will reach a maximum.

What to do

By taking the pulse rate at rest, the students will have a base line from which to work and can say if their pulse has increased after exercise. Different exercises will cause the heart to beat at different rates, depending on how strenuous the activity is.

Comparing the time expended on the exercise with the pulse rate will give more accurate results.

Encourage the students to see what happens to their pulse once they stop exercising as well. They could think about why their pulse returns to normal.

⚠️ Take the precautions you would take with any physical activity, and do not involve any students who do not normally do P.E.

What you need

- stopwatches

If you have access to a heart monitor or a pulse monitor, use it to check the data.

What to check

Students will need to use the stopwatches to time the exercise carefully as well as for counting their pulse. Taking the pulse from the same place each time keeps it fair. The exercise obviously needs to be kept the same.

The students will need to take an average of the pulse rates they take, either from the different people exercising or over the three times they take the pulse.

Support

If timing the exercise or timing and counting is a problem, let the whole class do the investigation at the same time, with you timing. Working with a partner to count the pulse rate will help students to count accurately.

Extend

All students should be able to say that the more you exercise the faster your heart rate becomes. They should also understand that the more you exercise, the longer it takes the pulse to return to normal.

Some groups could do different exercises and then place all the pulse rates on one graph to show which exercise makes the heart rate increase fastest. This is a challenging exercise.

What did you find? WS 13 WS 14

Record

The students could use WS 13 to record their measurements.

They could convert their recorded data into a graph. As they will have timed the exercise they could produce a line graph of their results.

Alternatively, they could use Class 5E's data given in the *Student Book* and on WS 14. This data is best presented as a bar chart, as it is not continuous.

Present

Ask students to present their findings in groups. If they used a heart or pulse monitor, they can compare their results with the monitors. The students should also include their table of results and charts. Can they tell the story of the chart or graph and draw conclusions?

Display on the wall a large graph of every person's resting pulse rate.

Can you do better?

Ask students to review how good their evidence was. *Is the evidence conclusive?* As the same thing happened to everyone, the evidence is conclusive.

Show the students Class 5E's results in the *Student Book*. Class 5E has decided to change the exercise, so cannot draw a line graph. This might lead them to conclude that their evidence is not conclusive, as there are other exercises they could do.

Class 5E could also have suggested changing the timing for the same exercise as an improvement.

Now predict

Class 5A should be informed about the heart speeding up and then slowing down as the runner starts to run, runs and then stops. The ability to sketch a graph of the predicted results is quite hard for this age group, but not impossible. You could provide them with some examples of graphs and ask them to predict which they think is closest or which it definitely isn't, to support their own graph drawing. They would then need to explain why they think it is this shape.

Class 5G will need to check their results to ensure they are accurate by taking pulse rates more than once. By taking the pulse of several people, you are making the evidence more secure.

Other ideas

Pulses

Let the students test their pulse rate in different places to check that it is the same throughout their body.

Leaflet

Encourage the students to produce a leaflet explaining why it is important to look after your heart.

Uninterrupted flow

Use the washing-up bottles to show what happens if you have a 'furred-up' artery. Use some plasticine to block up part of the bottle top and observe the difference in blood flow.

ICT ideas

If you have access to a microphone, record the heart sounds as the students are doing the investigation. This audio record of what happens as you exercise could then be incorporated into a presentation.

At home

Ask the students to do the same activity at home, but this time they should count their breaths for one minute before the exercise and for one minute afterwards. What do they notice? Why?

Plenary

Return to the original challenge of what affects pulse rate. The students should all be able to summarize that the more you exercise the faster your heart rate and the longer it takes to return to normal.

Unit 2: Keeping healthy – Drugs and you

The objectives for this lesson are that students should be able to:

- Learn why tobacco is not good for them and that it contains addictive substances

- Produce a presentation on smoking and what the risks include

- Find out why it is better to never start taking harmful drugs

- Understand the difference between medicines and drugs.

SB pp.20–21   *Starter*

- Discuss the effects smoking and solvents have on the body, including smell, strains and appearance. Some students may not be aware of the dangers of drugs such as solvents – and it is your professional judgement whether it is appropriate to introduce this area.

Explain

All change

Tobacco use is a tricky issue. Look at the statistics. Consider a thousand students in the age range you teach. As many as six may die in road accidents, but if all smoked, 250 would eventually die of smoking-related diseases. Consider the power of the big drug and tobacco industries, which embraces sports sponsorship and association. Remind students of tobacco's effects on teeth, skin and hair. Smoking is not cheap. Smoking for life costs the same as a Ferrari, or ten amazing holidays.

Handle tobacco education with care. Remember that in many families, smoking is taken for granted and that statements that smoking inevitably leads to lung cancer can cause students unnecessary anxiety when they look at their parents' habits.

Nicotine

Nicotine is the addictive substance in tobacco. Tobacco contains 6800 other substances. It has many physical effects. Tar accumulation in the lungs prevents oxygen absorption, and so leaves smokers short of breath. It kills the tiny hairs or cilia in the throat which remove sticky mucus. This mucus drains into the lungs. Smokers often

have a hacking cough first thing in the morning as they try to remove the accumulated mucus.

Not looking so good

The risks of dying of lung cancer are 22 times higher for male smokers and 12 times higher for female smokers than for non-smokers. Smokers are at increased risk of cancer of the larynx, oral cavity, oesophagus, bladder, kidney, and pancreas.

Smoking also causes a fivefold increase in the risk of dying from chronic bronchitis and emphysema, and a twofold increase in deaths from diseases of the heart and coronary arteries. It increases the risk of stroke by 50 per cent – 40 per cent among men and 60 per cent among women. There is clear evidence that smoking during pregnancy can reduce birth weight and can damage babies. There have been suggested links between homes with smokers and cot deaths.

Things to do   WS 15

Don't quit, just don't start

Give the students information to sort and present. Ask them to produce a presentation on their information so that Dr Quitit will know what to say, using WS 15.

Dig deeper

Students have the oppotunity to find out more about addiction, what it is and how it works.

I wonder…

Child-proof caps prevent accidental harm from overdosing. Explain to students that prescribed medicines, dispensed by a pharmacist and administered by a competent adult in the correct dose and at the right intervals, are the correct way to fight illness.

Did you know?

Smokers may try to stop. Many aids are available – including patches, tablets and hypnosis – to help people stop. Nicotine patches are small, nicotine-containing adhesive disks that are applied to the skin. The nicotine is slowly absorbed through the skin and enters the blood stream. The dose is gradually reduced. Nicotine gum works in a similar way, providing small doses of nicotine when chewed.

Nicotine is an addictive drug, and giving up this addiction is a struggle. Some are successful. But as numbers of smokers in developed countries fall, the numbers of smokers in developing countries is growing. Tobacco companies have shifted their emphasis to the developing world.

Other ideas
WS 16

Drug education

If you feel inadequate in this area, request support from health professionals. Drug education is a difficult issue. The 'shock' approach is common, using images such as those of dead addicts. So is the 'information' approach that tells young people the facts.

Students can be taught to refuse drugs. They can be shown famous or popular people as part of a lifestyle approach. They can be offered other, more acceptable risks – physical dangers, for example. They can have their self-esteem boosted so that they do not feel the need to take drugs. Peer tutoring can help, where students are taught by others of their own age or a little older – maybe through drama.

Staying healthy

Ask the students to produce a poster or leaflet on the effects of drugs on the body and why addictive drugs must be avoided/refused, using WS 16. They could collect information from the Internet or other sources.

Just say NO!

Ask students to make some simple rules for staying healthy – dos and don'ts. How can they stay fit? What actions are likely to make them healthy?

Ask the students to describe the medicines they have taken, when and how. Ask them to explain why medicines have to be handled with care, and to devise ways of keeping medicines safely. *Why are medicine cabinets usually high up on the wall? If a few tablets can do us good, why is it harmful to take a lot more?*

Challenge stereotypes of health and fitness. We don't all have to be ace sportspeople. You can be relatively fit when old or disabled. Investigate the Paralympics and other events where disability is no bar to fitness.

Look at tobacco smoking. *Why do people smoke? What body systems are harmed by smoking? Why is this?* Investigate smoking and its effects on the human body. *What does it do to you? How can people give up? What can smoking do to the teeth and lungs?*

Ask the students to label a picture of the chest and chest organs to show where and how tobacco smoking is harmful.

It may be appropriate to explore the ways that different drugs can affect you, what it means to become addicted and the ways that people try to break addiction. The students might investigate one addictive drug and describe the symptoms and effect to the rest of the class. Choose drugs which the students may be likely to come across. In this, as in all the drug-related activities, involve responsible health professionals.

Presentation

Ask the students to imagine they are doctors, and to prepare a presentation on what they have learned about the dangers of smoking and other drugs.

At home

This is a good topic for home research, but beware of students giving unnecessary concern to close relatives who smoke.

Plenary

Review what has been learned. Ask the students to come up with a personal five-point plan for staying healthy and free of addiction.

Unit 2: Keeping healthy – Unit 2: Review

The objectives for this lesson are that students should be able to:

- Check what they have learned about keeping healthy in this Unit

- Find out how they are working towards, within and beyond the Grade 5 level.

Expectations

Students working towards Grade 5 level will:

- Identify some foods needed for a healthy and varied diet and some harmful effects of drugs.

- Recognize that pulse rate is a measure of how fast the heart is beating.

- Make measurements of pulse rate.

- Present their data in graphs with help.

In addition, students working within Grade 5 level will:

- Identify the components of a healthy and varied diet and describe how an idea about the effect of diet on health was tested.

- Recognize that during exercise the heart beats faster to take blood more rapidly to the muscles.

- Make careful measurements of pulse rate and recognize the need to repeat measurements when evaluating their data.

- Represent these in suitable graphs and explain what the graphs show.

Further to this, students working beyond Grade 5 level will also:

- Explain some early evidence for the effect of diet on health.

- Explain why repeated measurements of pulse rate should be made.

- Explain why it is important to test the effects of exercise on the pulse rate of several people.

- Put their data into lines graphs independently.

- Use and explain repeated data and evaluate how good it is.

Heinemann Explore Science

Check-up

Discuss with students the different ideas they have to tell the runners in the cross-country race.

The runners will be breathing heavily to increase the oxygen going into their blood. The reason they can hear their heart pounding is that the pulse is beating strongly, so producing a throbbing that is in the pulse of the temples. Bone conducts sound very well, so the ears pick up the sound.

The heart is needed to pump the blood around to the muscles; they need the oxygen it carries to allow them to work properly. Without the oxygen the muscles will ache.

When they stop running, their heart rates will gradually slow down.

Assessment   WS 17   WS 18

Use the Unit 2 assessment on WS 17 and WS 18 to check the students' understanding of the content of the Unit. The answers are given below.

Answers

Unit 2 assessment 1

1   Your heart is in the centre of your chest, under your ribs.

2   Get hot, sweat and feel tired, muscles ache. Heart beats faster and breathe faster/harder

3   **a**   60
    b   Beat faster, increased rate
    c   30 minutes. Heartbeat begins to decrease after 30 minutes

Unit 2 assessment 2

4   Smoking means you can't breather properly, get coughs, lungs clogged, possible illness.

5   Heart ⟍ ⟋ Carries oxygen around the body
    Blood ⟋⟍ Breathe air, exchange oxygen and carbon dioxide
    Lungs ⟋ ⟍ Pumps blood around the body

6   Athletes are very fit, do lots of exercise, their hearts are used to/adapted to exercise.

Name: _____ Date: _____

WS 17

Unit 2 assessment 1

1 Where in your body is your heart? _____

2 Describe two changes you notice about your body when you exercise.
_____

3 The graph shows how heartbeat changes when you exercise. Use it to answer the questions below.

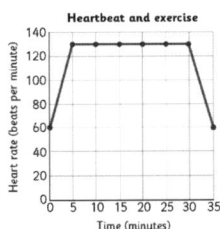

Heartbeat and exercise

Heart rate (beats per minute) vs Time (minutes)

a) What was your heart rate before you started running?
_____ beats per minute

b) What happened to your heart rate in the first five minutes that you were running?
_____

c) How long did you run for? How do you know?
_____

Unit 2: Keeping healthy   17

Name: _____ Date: _____

WS 18

Unit 2 assessment 2

4 Why does smoking make a football player less fit?
_____
_____
_____

5 Match up the body part and its function.

Heart   Carries oxygen around the body

Blood   Breathe in air, exchange oxygen
                         and carbon dioxide

Lungs
                         Pumps blood around the body

6 The hearts of athletes return to their resting heart rate very quickly after exercise. Explain why that happens.
_____
_____
_____

18   Heinemann Explore Science Grade 5

The answer!

Refer back to the original question on what the doctor might ask someone to do if they are overweight and smoke. If they are overweight, they will probably be eating either too much or the wrong type of foods. Also, they may not be taking sufficient exercise, so will need to start taking more. Gentle exercise will slowly introduce the heart to working harder and reduce the chance of a heart attack. If they smoke, as they exercise they will find breathing difficult and start to cough as mucus is clogging their lungs. As soon as they stop smoking, they will start to get better as the cilia recover and work again and their lungs will be cleaned.

And finally...

Create a large display of the students' results from the pulse rate and exercise enquiry with a student-sized diagram of the body showing a heart and the blood vessels.

A display of the leaflets that the students have produced on either drugs or a healthy diet or lifestyle will show what they have learned.

New International Edition

Unit 3: Life cycles

The objectives for this Unit are that students should be able to:

- Describe the conditions that plants and animals need to survive

- Understand that all living organisms grow and reproduce

- Find out that each living organism goes through a life cycle

- Display results of scientific investigations in various ways, including bar charts.

SB p.23   Science background

Sexual reproduction involves the combining of genetic material from both parents to produce a new individual. It happens in both plants and animals. Sometimes the product of the process doesn't even look alive. Some students believe that hens' eggs and seeds are not alive, though in changed circumstances either may produce new life.

Research has shown that younger students may believe new life is formed from components or parts; new human babies manufactured 'in a mummy's tummy' from bits; chicks assembled from kits of legs, wings, head and body floating around inside the egg.

Life follows a distinct cycle, with birth, growing and reproductive phases, always ending in death. Understandably, metamorphosis – the spectacular life cycle in which animals undergo huge changes – caterpillar to butterfly, tadpole to frog – catches the imagination; but most animals produce young that resemble the adult – even those that go through partial metamorphosis – a 'nymph' stage.

Flowering plants reproduce with seeds; other plants commonly use spores. Many students have had little experience of harvesting and growing seeds, and few have had the opportunity to see a flowering plant go through its whole life cycle.

Language

| Fertilization | The combining of sperm and egg or pollen and ovum. |
| Germination | When a seed sends out its first root. |

Ovary	Contains the female ovule of a flowering plant.
Ovule	Female element of a flowering plant.
Ovum	A single egg within the ovary
Pollen	A fine powder that contains the male element of a flowering plant.
Pollination	Transfer of pollen from one flower usually to the stigma of another.
Stamen	Male reproductive part of a flower that produces pollen.
Stigma	Female part of the flower that receives the pollen.

The Words to learn list on page 23 of the *Student Book* can be used to make a classroom display.

Resources

- *Life Cycles* Reader.

- Hand lenses or magnifiers or microscopes could be used, but students will need time to learn how to use them properly.

- A selection of seeds which have different properties for dispersal. Include some edible fruits, some that are windblown, some that explode and some that float.

- Large simple flowers.

- A sharp knife or scalpel (only for use by the teacher).

- Seeds for germinating.

- Small pots.

- Cotton wool.

- Measuring devices.

Bright ideas

- If you have one, use a digital camera to record the germination of seeds, or a video camera or digital microscope on time-lapse. You could use a still camera for the measuring activity on plants and light too.

- Make sure you use quick-germinating seeds. Choose something that will produce a flower, if possible. Continue to grow the resulting seeds to recreate a life cycle. Gather together examples of a plant at different stages of its life.

- Ask the students to start collecting some photos of an adult member of their family that were taken at various times during their life. Ensure they ask permission from the adult first.

- If you have one, a light sensor could be used to test how much light actually gets to the seeds that are left to germinate, to prove that they can be left in the dark.

Knowledge check

- Remind students that both plants and animals are living organisms. Recap 'Mr Green' to establish the seven processes that living things go through.

  Movement

  Reproduction

  Growth

  Respiration – getting energy from food

  Excretion – getting rid of waste

  Excitation – response to a stimulus

  Nutrition – using food

- Students should know from topics in Grade 3 that animals need food and that plants make their own food from the Sun, but also produce food for us to eat, either leaves, roots, stems or fruits. Plants need warmth, light, water and air to grow well.

- Students will think that because plants need light, seeds will also need light to germinate. Although the activity in 'Germinating seeds' is similar to one carried out in Grade 3, the aim of it is to challenge the students' thinking.

- Most students will be aware that they grow up and become adults. They may not be aware that all other animals do the same, unless they have seen it happen to a pet. They may also be unaware that plants go through a similar process of growing up and reproducing.

Skills check

Students need to:

- measure volume, temperature and distance

- make observations and comparisons

- suggest explanations for their investigations, using their background knowledge.

Some students will:

- name the structures and functions of all parts of a flower

- explain why it is important to use more than one seed in an investigation on germination.

Links to other subjects

Literacy: Read and following simple instructions, e.g. setting up the germinating seeds enquiry. Labelling a diagram, e.g. the flower structure.

Numeracy: Measuring volume and temperature. Comparing using standard units. Organizing and interpreting simple data in bar graphs or line graphs.

ICT: Using a digital camera, video or digital microscope. Using a multi-media package to combine text and graphics to make a presentation.

Art: Exploring line, shape, colour and texture in natural forms.

PSHE: Discussing the process of growing up and changing.

Let's find out...

The Unit opens with this question:

Salmon live in rivers and the sea. After years at sea they swim back to the same river where they were born. After thousands of miles in the sea, then upstream against the river, many become exhausted. They struggle on until they succeed or die. Why do the salmon return to their birthplace, even if some die?

Discuss the question. Throughout the topic the students will learn about the life cycles of both animals and plants. They will come to realize that animals grow older and often reproduce young. Many will do this as part of an instructive or built-in pattern that they can't change.

43

Unit 3: Life cycles – The Sun's light

The objectives for this lesson are that students should be able to:

- Understand what the Sun is and why we need it to survive

- Learn how plants use light and how much they need

- Measure the growth of two plants that were given different amounts of light

- Present their findings on how to keep a plant healthy.

SB pp.24–25 — *Starter*

Ask students to find a food chain that doesn't go back to a green plant and therefore not back to the Sun. Many things, even plastic, can be traced back to the Sun – showing its importance (e.g. plastic is made from oil, oil was made from small organisms which have died, that in turn got their energy from the Sun).

Provide a list of materials on the board, e.g. chicken, cotton socks, wooden table, plastic ruler, woollen jumper, string, etc. and ask students to come up with a way that they are all linked (all made with plant materials).

Explain

Light and energy

The Sun is a fiery ball of gas that is burning fiercely. This releases energy in the form of heat and light that travels through the vacuum of space and reaches the Earth. Other planets in our solar system are either too close to the Sun and are too hot for life, or too far away and therefore too cold and dark. The atmosphere around the Earth helps retain the Sun's heat. High levels of carbon dioxide and other 'greenhouse gases' increase the insulation and raise the Earth's temperature.

Plants and light

The opening paragraphs illustrate the importance of light and the energy it provides through plants. Plants trap the energy from sunlight with a chemical in the green part of their leaves, called chlorophyll (*chloro* means green or yellowish

green, and *phyllos* is Greek for leaf). The chlorophyll absorbs the light and, through a series of chemical reactions, turns the carbon dioxide from the air and the water from the ground into complex sugars which are stored as starch. This produces oxygen as a waste product which **all** living things need for respiration, including plants. This whole process is called photosynthesis. *Photo* means light and *synthesis* means to make, so it means 'making with light'.

The starch that the plant makes is stored either in its leaves, roots, stems or seeds, hence humans and other animals eating tubers and the roots of some plants e.g. potatoes, carrots, parsnips, etc.

Things to do

Growing upwards

Plants will grow towards the light to trap their energy to make their own food. You should see the plant in the cylinder growing much taller than the one in full light as it grows upwards towards the light. There will be other differences too. It may well become spindly and it will possibly have slightly more yellow leaves where the Sun doesn't get to them. You could ask the students to remember back to work they did in Grade 3 on covering a part of a leaf with foil and asking if they can use this to explain the differences between the plants.

They will need to decide on what kind of table to produce and how many columns to have. This is good practice.

Record

Other ways of recording and sharing this information include:

- cartoon strip of images

- digital photographs taken at regular intervals

- producing a graph of the tabulated results. *Is the data continuous? What type of graph will you need to produce?*

Other ways of finding out could include putting the entire plant in a dark place, or covering up just one leaf. You could try pulling all the leaves off the plant to observe how well it grows without them, showing that the plant needs the green parts for photosynthesis, but this is destructive as it will probably kill the plant.

Support

Discuss the type of table needed and model the drawing of it with students, e.g. 2 columns and then ask them to complete the headings of plant position and height.

Extension

Students decide on their own table design and also consider the importance of accurate measuring.

Discuss whether they would need to measure every day? Why not?

I wonder...

This is quite an easy experiment to set up with different colour light bulbs or with filters/colour transparencies or even some sweet wrappers over the light bulb.

> ⚠ Be careful not to melt the transparencies or sweet wrappers.

If you set up the plants in cardboard boxes and exclude as much light as possible you should be able to record the results. Don't forget to compare this to a plant grown in 'normal' conditions.

Questions to probe the student's understanding might include: *Why isn't this really a fair test?; What could be the problems with the experiment?* (can't exclude all natural light). *Are all the plants individuals?* (Might need a bigger sample size etc.)

Dig deeper

Students could find out more about whether plants can grow and be green without sunlight.

Did you know?

The oceans are very little explored. Over 70 per cent of the Earth is covered in water and 85 per cent of all plant life is found in the seas and oceans.

Other ideas

Are all plants green?

Why are some plants not green, e.g. some of the red leaved varieties? How do they use sunlight? Compare and contrast them with a green plant. The students could also compare their growth in a similar way to the main activity or even the I wonder... activity to see if different coloured leaves grow better in different lights.

Under the sea

How do plants under the sea get their light? This would be a research activity that could be presented in the form of an information booklet, PowerPoint presentation or a poster.

Presentation

Prepare an instruction page for keeping a really healthy plant, or pretend to be a botanist explaining to a younger class how a plant needs light to grow well, by means of an interview about a new plant that has been discovered in the jungle.

At home

Carry out a survey of plants at home. *Where do they grow best?*

At this stage students should be drawing their own ways of presenting evidence, hence no WS.

Plenary

Play the challenge game from the start, even if played previously. Ask students to come up with ideas of things that *don't* need light at the start.

OR

Carry out a 'what if...? *What if the sunlight was weaker?*

Unit 3: Life cycles – New life

The objectives for this lesson are that students should be able to:

- Understand that pollination is the transfer of pollen from one plant to another

- Explain why insects are important to plants and pollination

- Find out what attracts insects to plants

- Draw and describe the parts of a flower and what they do.

SB pp.26–27

Starter

- Describe what pollination is – when pollen from the male part of one flower is transferred to the female part of another.

- Show illustrations of two flowers and ask the students to think about how the two flowers are pollinated. One flower should be pollinated by insects. It should have large petals and a central stigma with stamen around it.

- The other flower should be wind pollinated, with the sexual parts of the flower hanging outside the 'petals'. Point out that flowers that are wind pollinated tend to be dull and have no scent. They have no need to attract insects to do their pollinating.

- Make the difference in type even clearer by taking in some wind-pollinated grass flowers and some quite fragrant or colourful flowers, such as roses or tulips.

Explain

Flowers are useful

Share a range of flowers and arrange them in order of beauty. Although this is subjective, it could be a useful discussion tool to help articulate ideas and preferences. Students could go on to produce an image/picture of the flower that they think is most beautiful to them and label with annotations to explain why.

Pollination

Students may have seen bees and other insects landing on flowers. *What is the insect doing?* It is collecting nectar from which it will make honey or use to feed itself. As it pushes past the stamens to get to the nectar, the pollen sticks to the hairs on its body and legs. When it flies to a new flower, the pollen brushes on the stigma and stays there. More pollen is collected from the new flower, and so the insect continues the cross-pollination process.

Students can find it quite hard to distinguish between pollination and fertilization. Accentuate the word 'pollen' in pollination (although it isn't spelled the same) to help the students remember that it involves transfer of pollen from one plant to another.

Attractive to insects

Try standing further back and discovering which colour of flower can be seen from furthest away. The brightest may attract more insects. Try smelling flowers from further distances too.

Fertilization

Fertilization is the combining of a male and a female cell nucleus. A nucleus is the part of a cell that contains the genetic information for a new living thing, i.e. a rose and no other type of plant will grow from a rose seed. The same process happens in animals – a sperm and an egg join together. In plants, male and female elements in the pollen and ovule combine.

Things to do

What is in a flower?

A flower has both male and female parts. This means that if it isn't cross-pollinated, there is a chance of self-pollination. During cross-pollination, a flower is pollinated by the pollen from a different flower of the same species.

Obtain some large, simple flowers such as tulips, daffodils, hibiscus or lilies (often lilies bought from florists have had the stamens cut out because the pollen stains) for this activity. Encourage the students to remove the petals gently, leaving the stamen and stigma intact. These can be placed in a circle on a piece of paper. A 2D picture of their flower can be built up, with the petals on the outside. By carefully removing the stamens and stigma from the flower, these can also be placed in position. Use a scalpel or a sharp knife yourself to cut the ovary in half to show the students the ovules inside. Fix the whole flower to a piece of paper with sticky tape or book covering material.

Record

Once the students have built up their flower, ask them to label it, in a similar way to the one in the *Student Book*. Ask them to annotate what each part does, i.e. petals attract insects, anthers produce pollen, etc.

Support

Ensure all plant parts are displayed before more are removed.

Extend

Some students will be able to recognize the male and female parts in more complicated flowers. Show other flowers and ask the students to identify the different parts.

I wonder...

The scent of the Rafflesia flower attracts mainly flies as the rotting flesh smell is similar to rotting food. The flies transfer the pollen from one flower to the next.

Dig deeper

Students have the opportunity to find out about methods of pollination and what happens to the flower after pollination.

Did you know?

Facts here remind students how small pollen grains are.

White or pale yellow flowers reflect the most light, so they are more visible at night. This means moths may be attracted to them, and can act as pollinators.

Most flowers and leaves assume a slightly dropped position at night, called nyctitropism, so are not pollinated at night.

Flowers that attract bees and butterflies tend to be blue, yellow or pink. You could test this by carrying out a survey of flowers visited by insects over the course of a lesson.

Other ideas   WS 19   WS 20

Life of a plant

Ask the students to draw a labelled picture of each stage in the cycle of a plant. Alternatively they could complete WS 19 and WS 20.

Fieldwork

Take the students out to any area which has flowers, wild flowers or 'weeds'. Observe the insects that visit the area. Collect the data in a table and produce a graph or pictogram. What colour flowers attract most bees?

Pollen grains

Use a hand lens or a microscope to observe pollen grains from different flowers, e.g. lily, tulip and grasses. Students should see pollen of different sizes and shapes. Compare these to wind-pollinated pollen, which is much smaller. Use pictures to show how the pollen attaches itself to the insect.

Presentation

Let the students pretend to be gardening experts, explaining why you shouldn't kill all the insects in your garden. If they have used a video recorder to observe the insects on flowers, they can incorporate this into a PowerPoint presentation to accompany their talk.

At home

Ask the students to investigate other ways in which plants reproduce, other than pollination and seed production. For example, strawberries are propagated by runners, potatoes by tubers.

Alternatively, ask them to design a flower to attract a bee, choosing the colour and shape carefully. Beelines on some petals direct the bees to the nectaries.

Plenary

Show some pictures of passion fruit flowers, small buds and then passion fruit. If you can get fruit with leaves on, or the remains of the flower showing, use them to illustrate that the flower is pollinated to produce a seed. In fact, the seeds are inside the passion fruit, and the fruit is the ovary.

47

Unit 3: Life cycles – Fruits and seeds

The objectives for this lesson are that students should be able to:

- Realize that seeds can grow into new plants

- Understand what the seed of a flowering plant is for

- Learn how plants scatter their seeds and why they need to do this

- Examine seeds that they have collected to see how they are dispersed.

SB pp.28–29   *Starter*

- Show a variety of seeds, including some that we can eat. Remind students that some plants produce seeds and fruits that we eat, e.g. apples, tomatoes, cherries, peaches, oranges, strawberries, peas, beans, coconuts, peanuts, walnuts, etc. Discuss which part of the plant we eat, if any. Cut some soft fruits in half to observe where the seeds are. Avoid seedless grapes or oranges. *Why do plants have seeds? Are they tasty to eat? Does the plant only produce them for us?*

- Show some weed seeds that we don't eat, similar to goose-grass or broom seeds in their pods, which are dispersed by explosion and flowers such as poppies, which are wind dispersed as the seeds are very small and contained in a rattle-like seed head. Discuss with the students how each could be dispersed and what indicators they can find to help them decide.

> ⚠ Some students are allergic to nuts. They must not handle nuts of any sort.

Explain

Seed dispersal

This entire section follows on from the previous pollination and fertilization section. It is important for the students to realize that once fertilization has taken place, the seed then develops in the ovary of the plant. Students need to understand *why* the seeds can't just fall next to their parents to grow.

One student acts as the parent plant and drops 'seeds' as pieces of card from outstretched arms. Where each piece of card lands, a new plant grows, i.e. a student stands there. Each 'new plant' then drops their 'seeds'. The accumulation of pieces of card should demonstrate that the plants from dropped seeds are very crowded. *What do plants need to grow well? What will happen if they are crowded together?* Invite the students to throw their pieces of card as far as possible. *What happens?* They are more spread out, so should grow better.

How seeds travel

How else can the students think of spreading their seeds? For instance, other students could carry them, they could throw them, the wind could carry them, etc. Point out that this is what a plant does.

Use a digital microscope to show some of the hooks on seeds dispersed by animals. Otherwise, use hand-lenses. Velcro mimics the hooks on some seeds. Let the students compare Velcro hooks with seeds.

Other ways of transporting the seeds link to the starter. Some seeds are dispersed by fresh and salt water.

Things to do

What's inside?

Large beans and chick peas are needed for this activity. Soak them in advance to soften the skin.

A seed has 'seed leaves' or cotyledons that are food stores. Some seeds have two food stores with a tiny root and shoot hidden between them, waiting to grow. These are called dicotyledon plants. Some plants only have one and are called monocotyledon plants. These can be identified by the leaf veins along the length of the leaf, rather than branching. A seed does not need to make food to grow as it has its own supply. Only when it develops leaves does a plant use light for photosynthesis.

> ⚠ Remind the students to wash their hands after handling seeds.

Record

The students should draw and label a large bean to show the tiny root and shoot.

Support

You may need to help some students to break open the bean seed, as it is quite delicate. Provide some whole seeds and some already split in half.

Extend

All students should realize that seeds can grow into a new plant.

Some students will be able to recognize a small root and shoot in other seeds. Provide some chick peas and runner beans for them to split and observe.

Know your seeds

This activity allows the students to start to group seeds based on their features and produce either a set of criteria so they can assign unknown seeds to their correct groups, or to attempt to produce a branching key. Branching keys are covered in Grade 6.

I wonder...

A Satsuma orange will float in water. The skin has tiny air pockets in it that are sealed. The peel will float by itself, but the fruit inside will sink if the peel is removed.

Dig deeper

Students have the opportunity to find out more about plants and seeds. Looking at and handling real fruits and seeds allows the students to understand clearly how seeds are dispersed.

Did you know?

These facts show that seeds come in different sizes and are dispersed in a variety of ways.

Other ideas

Oranges and lemons

Plants produce food for us to eat, and some of them are medicinal as well as tasty. In the past sailors rarely had fruit and vegetables to eat on board ship, so they didn't have a source of vitamin C. James Lind discovered the link between diet and scurvy, and sailors were given citrus fruit to eat to keep them healthy at sea. The popularity of oranges and lemons grew among richer populations. Rather than import the fruit

at great expense from hot countries, in colder countries they were grown in heated 'orangeries'.

How far?

Use some of the seeds you have brought in to see how far you can make them disperse. Put the discs from a paper punch in a balloon. Inflate the balloon. Tie it off. When you burst it the discs will be dispersed. Try putting the fruits and seeds into water. *Do any of the seeds 'cling' to fur? What happens if the seed isn't suited to the method?*

Survey

If you have a garden, look for seedlings under parent plants and measure the height of the seedlings against the distance from the parent. The further away from the parent the seed landed and germinated, the bigger the seedling should be. Of course, it could have germinated earlier. *Why would this have happened?* (Access to more resources needed for germination.)

Digestion

Discuss how a fruit which contains a seed can survive travelling through an animal's or human's insides. Remind students that we have acid in our stomachs. Place a peach in vinegar and leave it for a week to see what happens to the 'stone' seed inside. The flesh should end up as mush but the stone should still be intact. It could survive stomach acids.

Presentation

Encourage the students to prepare a series of short video clips of how seeds are dispersed, illustrating wind, water and explosion.

At home

Ask the students to look closely at the vegetables and fruit they eat at home. How do they think they were dispersed? Students complete WS 21.

Plenary

Show the students an unusual fruit. Ask them where the seeds are and how they think they were dispersed. A strawberry is a good example. The animal-dispersed seeds are on the outside.

49

Unit 3: Life cycles – Investigating seed shapes

The objectives for this lesson are that students should be able to:

- Discover what shape carries a seed furthest in the air

- Find out how to make seeds travel far in a fair way

- Make predictions on which seed will travel furthest

- Evaluate how to accurately measure their design and their results.

SB pp.30–31

Starter

- This challenge is based on one method of dispersal. It is the most convenient to experiment with, although you could try the 'explosion' method with elastic bands and/or catapults and different sizes of elastic bands or seeds. However, there are more risks of injury involved with this as an activity.

- Take in some flying seeds, or ask the students to bring some in. Let them have plenty of fun throwing them into the air and watching them spin! Encourage them to use this time to think about how to make the seeds travel far and in a fair way. What do you notice about the single seeds with only one wing? They tend to spin faster and land sooner than double and triple-winged seed clusters.

- Alternatively, show a photo of flying seeds and discuss how the seeds are able to travel some distance from the parent plant.

- Winged seeds are often known as 'helicopters'. However, a helicopter has an engine; winged seeds are gyrocopters; they spin or 'gyrate' their way to the ground.

The challenge

Read the What to do and conversations on page 30 in the *Student Book*. Discuss what Class 5 wants to investigate. From the Starter activity the students should realize that the student complaining about

having only one wing is quite justified. They might also notice that one student suggests changing two factors simultaneously which doesn't make the test fair. The third suggestion is invalid as it suggests an investigation which isn't fair.

What to do

Changing the wing shape produces words (wing shape) and number (time taken to fall) and so is recorded on a bar chart. Changing the length of the wing and recording the time produces two sets of figures (continuous data) and so a line graph.

What you need

WS 22

- WS 22 with the templates of the spinners

- stopwatches

- ideally, a video camera to film the spinners as they fall – this is helpful if you can display passing time on the film.

What to check

The spinners should all be the same shape. If you use the templates on WS 22, they will be four times as long (in total) as they are wide, i.e. a 6 cm spinner wing, will be 12 cm long in total and 3 cm wide.

Support

Pre-cut some of the spinner shapes from the templates to ensure that they are the same shape and design.

Timing the fall is quite difficult with the smaller spinners as they fall very quickly. The students might need help reading the stopwatches.

Extend

All students should be able to say which size of spinner took the longest to fall. Gravity (a constant) is pulling the spinner downwards. But air resistance (which varies with wing size) is slowing the fall.

More able students could predict how the line graph would look with smaller or larger wings.

Some students could experiment with the shape of the wing, or the width of the wing, or add paper clip weights.

What did you find? WS 23

Record

The students could record their results on WS 23. They could convert their recorded data into a graph. As an alternative, they could use Class 5's idealized data given in the *Student Book*. This data will produce a line graph.

Present

If the students used the video camera to film the fall of their spinners, they can use this to check their timing. The film could be used as part of a PowerPoint presentation to show how the length of wing affects the fall. They will also be able to watch how the spinner moves through the air and describe it.

Can you do better? WS 24

Show the students Class 5's report on WS 24. Read it together. *Were the instructions detailed enough? Did the fair test state everything that was kept the same? Are the results written correctly?*

Did the students evaluate their investigation by saying what they could do better next time? This is an important skill to introduce. The students need to start being critical of their own procedure and say how they would do the investigation differently to get better results. Repeating the investigation to check their results are accurate is always a good suggestion. This also helps to eliminate, or even spot, errors. The repetitions can either be used to check the results or an average taken to use the results quantitatively.

Now predict

The students should be able to tell that the seeds that stay in the air longest will be blown the furthest, so these would be best for a large plant. A smaller plant does not need so much space to grow, so the seeds will not need to be dispersed so far.

Class 5J's seeds will travel a long way because the seeds themselves are smaller or weigh less.

Other ideas

Size of seed

The students could repeat the investigation they have carried out, timing the fall, but changing the mass on the bottom. Instead of having just one paper clip, they could change the number of paper clips or the mass of plasticine.

Other methods of dispersal

The students could explore other methods of dispersal, e.g. in design and technology they could design a catapult to create an explosion of seeds. Or they could look at how seeds with hooks are transported by animals, or investigate Velcro, which imitates this mechanism.

ICT ideas

Information from the activity could be entered in a graphing program and used to draw a range of different types of graph. Remind students that 'size of wing' (the independent variable) should be on the x-axis, and 'time to fall' (the dependent variable) on the y-axis. All graphs need a title and labels on both axes.

If you are able to 'capture' the pictures from the video to show how a spinner falls, print them alongside the students' reports.

At home

Ask the students to make a list of seeds and fruits they eat at home, and say how they are dispersed.

Alternatively, they could drop different types of seeds and see which lands first. *Why is the apple not suited to wind dispersal?*

Plenary

It is essential that students explain their discoveries, despite the fact that they might not be able to explain why a spinner with a bigger surface area falls more slowly. Encourage the students to think about how they run with their shirts flapping open and then with their shirts done up. It is hard to run with flapping shirts as there is more air resistance.

Unit 3: Life cycles – Germinating seeds

The objectives for this lesson are that students should be able to:

- Learn that seeds don't require the same conditions as plants for growth
- Identify all the conditions a seed needs to germinate
- Plan and carry out a scientific investigation to measure seed germination
- Draw a conclusion from the evidence they gather.

SB pp.32–33   Starter

- Remind students of the conditions that plants require to grow well. If you can, take in some healthy plants and some less healthy, i.e. lacking in water and light, from previous teaching. The students should remember the conditions.
- Remind students that seeds do not need light to germinate. Show a photo of a bean starting to grow and explain that germination is the time when the seed sends out a tiny root and shoot to start growing into a plant. Show them some trays of seedlings at various stages of development to prove that they grow into plants.

The challenge

Read the What to do and conversations on page 32 in the *Student Book*. To illustrate the cartoon, set out the seeds and talk through the cartoon saying that your seeds 'aren't very happy'. *How can we make them 'happy'?* Discuss the different suggestions made by Class 5A. In fact, none of the suggestions on their own is a fair test, or at least the conditions are not stated fully enough for the class to ensure the investigation will be fair. The investigation needs to combine elements of all four ideas to test the conditions seeds require for germination.

What to do

The challenge is to identify what conditions a seed needs to germinate quickly. Encourage the students to suggest testing more than one seed. This will ensure a reliable set of results. Some seeds will not germinate as they may not be viable, or kept in the wrong conditions. Agree on

a set of growing conditions, e.g. 10 ml of water on a bed of cotton wool, room temperature and light. Change only one condition at a time.

What you need

- fast growing seeds, e.g. radish, cress, lettuce
- Petri dishes or trays lined with cotton wool
- a measuring cylinder
- water
- ideally, a digital camera or video camera to take time-lapse shots

What to check

The number of seeds must be kept the same. Class 5A have made no mention of this. This means their evidence is not completely reliable. Class 5A have tried to test all the conditions, but still have not mentioned a fair test. Your class needs to decide what information they are going to collect.

The results can be recorded in different ways. Simple results, using words and numbers, will produce a bar chart.

Checking the seeds every day and counting the number germinated in each area will produce two sets of figures and a line graph.

> ⚠ If you buy packets of seeds, check they are not treated with pesticides. Seeds from health food shops or suppliers for schools should be safe to handle.

Support

As the investigation involves leaving the seeds for up to 14 days to germinate, some students may lose interest. Checking the seeds every day will help maintain their interest, especially if the students not only record the results in a table, but also start the graph off on the first day and plot it every day. Create a large-scale graph on the wall for all the students to follow.

Extend

All students should recognize the conditions where seeds have germinated fastest.

Some students may be able to question how relevant the volume of water is, or the actual temperature.

What did you find? WS 25

Record

The students should use the table on WS 25 to record the number of seeds that have germinated each day. This table will produce a chart. As an alternative, they could use Class 5A's idealized data given in the *Student Book*. The data in this enquiry is not continuous so only a bar chart can be produced.

Present

Ask the students to pretend that they are a team of television gardening show presenters. Encourage them to use ICT and incorporate video footage of seeds growing, or time-lapse digital camera slides.

Can you do better?

Show the students Class 5A's results in the *Student Book*. Read them together. *Were Class 5A detailed enough in their observations? Did they conclude accurately from their evidence?* The students have made a prediction based on prior knowledge. They failed to record the number of seeds they used or the amount of water in each tray. They also haven't used all the evidence to conclude accurately or make any suggestions for further investigations.

Now predict

Class 5 will need to be told that the leaves require sunlight, but as a seed doesn't have any leaves it doesn't need light to grow. PowerPoint images of plants grown in different conditions and the recent seed experiment could help explain this.

Class 5K will need to place their seeds in a warm, damp place. Students with experience of cooler countries may mention a glasshouse at this point. An instruction leaflet will help focus as this has literacy links too.

Other ideas

Simple glasshouse

If students have used prior knowledge of glasshouses for Class 5K's seeds to germinate, try setting up some seeds to see if the warmer environment makes a difference. Placing cling film over a seed tray on a sunny window sill in the classroom makes a simple glasshouse.

Which way up?

Curl a sheet of paper towel around the inside of a small jar and pour some water in the bottom. Pack the jar with crumpled paper towel. Put bean seeds between the paper and the jar. Once the roots have started to appear, gently turn the seeds round so the root points upwards. Ask the students what they think will happen. Will the plants grow upside down? The root will curve to grow downwards again. It responds to gravity.

ICT ideas

Set up a video camera to take time-lapsed shots of seeds growing, or use a digital camera on time delay. This will produce a 'movie' of the seeds germinating.

Place some seeds under a digital microscope and set it on time lapse. This will show that the root grows first and then the shoot.

At home

Give the students a seed in a plastic pot to take home and ask them to germinate it and return the seedling to school at the end of the term.

Plenary

Recap why the seed doesn't need light, i.e. it has no leaves which need sunlight to photosynthesize.

Unit 3: Life cycles – Life cycles

The objectives for this lesson are that students should be able to:

- Understand how each species of plant and animal need to reproduce to survive

- Learn that every living thing has a life cycle and what one looks like

- Collect information on gestation periods for different animals and produce a graph to display their findings

- Discover how similar life cycles are between all living things.

SB pp.34–35   Starter

- Start with the human life cycle and ask students to draw or write the names of the stages that they will go through as they grow up. Then ask about other animals. *What stages do they go through?*

- Show a photo of a young kangaroo in its mother's pouch. *Why might kangaroos carry their young in a pouch?*

- Show students pictures of young animals to show how animals change. Remind students of the life cycles of plants. *What are the names of the stages? Are there the same stages in an animal life cycle?* There isn't any pollination, and some students will be unaware of fertilization within animals, but both animals and plants have young which grow older, reproduce and have young of their own.

- Show pictures of the stages of a human life cycle. Discuss the changes occurring to individuals.

- If the students have brought in pictures of themselves when they were younger, use them to show how they have changed as they have grown older. Start to place the pictures in order of age. *What other pictures do you need to create a complete life cycle?*

Explain

How species survive

Without reproduction, species would quickly die out. Organisms that are best suited to certain conditions survive. These produce offspring that are adapted to survive in turn.

Different organisms provide differing amounts of care to ensure the survival of their offspring. There are two general approaches to species survival. One is to produce a great many eggs and offspring, and hope that some reach adulthood. The other is to produce a small number of offspring, and protect and nurture them.

On and on and on...

Every living thing has a life cycle, although some seeds remain dormant for a large part of a plant life cycle.

The diagram in the *Student Book* shows the stages of the life cycle of a plant, without the key vocabulary. This could be added by the students.

Life cycle stages

The link between animals and plants is that they have a life cycle as they are living things. There is a basic life cycle (birth, growth, reproduction, death/birth etc.) but some organisms, plant or animal, have 'extra' phases or special names for different parts of their life cycles. Students could match any organism to it and then consider the 'extras'. Insects have 'pupae' and 'metamorphosis' which do not fit a basic life cycle.

Things to do   WS 26

The wheel of life

Either ask the students to collect the information themselves and produce a graph, or use WS 26 which includes a graph of the gestation periods of different animals.

Human life cycle

By placing the pictures in a circle, it is easy to see that the life cycle is continuous. However, young adult humans have babies and then live into old age so a circle does not accurately represent the human life cycle.

Record

In answering some of the questions, the students illustrate that they have interpreted the graph correctly.

1   A sheep gestates for 20 weeks; a horse for 44 weeks.

2   Human gestation is longer, by 26 weeks.

3   The animals vary in size.

4   Generally, the bigger the animal, the longer the gestation time.

Support

Explain gestation in terms of it being the length of time a baby spends inside its mother.

If students haven't brought in any pictures of themselves or family members, ask them to draw a self-portrait.

Extend

All students should be able to recognize that the bigger the animal, the longer the gestation time, in general.

Some students may be able to use the information on masses of animals to produce a bar chart of size against gestation time. Is there a pattern?

All students should recognize that as we grow up we need less help from our parents to do simple tasks. Most will notice that as we get older we can perform more difficult tasks.

Some students will be able to use different colours to write down things that their parents teach them and things they learn at school, distinguishing between skills that are essential for life and those needed to improve the quality of life.

I wonder...

Generally, people use not only looks to guess someone's age, but also how the person behaves. We may assess students' ages on their skills and understanding.

Dig deeper

Students have the opportunity to find out more about animal life cycles.

A baby spends about nine months inside its mother. An embryo is a baby between 0 and 8 weeks old inside the uterus. After this it is called a foetus, or fetus.

Did you know?

These facts remind students that different animals care for their young in different ways.

Kangaroos are marsupials. They give birth to their young alive, but very immature. The kangaroo gives birth when its baby is about 1 cm long. The baby then climbs into its mother's pouch and starts feeding from nipples in the pouch.

Other ideas

Happy families

Produce a table of animals' names and the name we give their offspring. *Are there any stages in between?* For example, horse: foal, filly, mare; cow: calf, heifer. Produce a set of cards with animal names on for the students to play a game similar to happy families.

Presentation

Ask students to pretend that they are primary school teachers explaining to younger students the life cycle of a plant. In groups, prepare a PowerPoint presentation, using pictures of plants taken at different stages. Help them to run the pictures into one another so that the plant looks as if it's growing.

At home   WS 27 WS 28

Ask the students to answer the questions about the family tree on WS 27 and to find out about their own family tree using WS 28.

Plenary

Show the students diagrams or pictures of various stages of an animal's life cycle, e.g. chicken, egg, hatchling, chick, pullet, chicken. Ask them to sort them into the correct order. Where should they start? They should realize that the cycle can start at any point. *What care does the chicken provide for its young? What skills have chicks learned as they have grown up? Who taught them?*

Unit 3: Life cycles – Unit 3: Review

The objectives for this lesson are that students should be able to:

- Check what they have learned about life cycles in this Unit

- Find out how they are working towards, within and beyond the Grade 5 level.

SB p.36 **Expectations**

Students working towards Grade 5 level will:

- Name the parts of a flower and explain how pollen and seeds are dispersed.

- Describe some of the conditions tested in investigating germination.

- Recognize some stages in the development of humans.

- Draw simple conclusions about their observations.

In addition, students working within Grade 5 level will:

- Explain the functions of some parts of a flower.

- Describe the processes of pollination, fertilization, seed dispersal and germination.

- Explain how to carry out a fair test to find the conditions necessary for germination.

- Describe the role of insects in pollination.

- Recognize that plants need energy from the Sun to grow.

- Recognize the slightly different growing requirements for germinating seeds.

- Explain that living things need to reproduce if the species is to survive.

- Recognize stages in the growth and development of humans.

- Make careful relevant observations and explain what these show.

- Identify factors to make a test fair.

Further to this, students working beyond Grade 5 level will also:

- Explain why it is important to use a number of seeds or plants in an investigation into growth or germination.

- Use their data to make clear explanations.

- Identify the factors in an investigation.

Check-up

Discuss the idea of keeping animals in a classroom with the students. Why might a same-sex pair prove easier to keep?

- If there is a female and a male then they will reproduce and have babies.

- Under ideal circumstances (limitless space, limitless food, no disease or predators) it takes a mouse about 19 days (3 weeks) to have a litter of babies. A mouse needs to be about 9 weeks old to reach an age where it can reproduce. So the first pair of mice will have a litter every 3 weeks. In a litter there are about 6 babies. This means that in 1 year the first pair will produce 104 mice! But the offspring will also be reproducing. The students could then produce a graph of the number of mice, i.e. 2 parents; 2 parents plus 6 offspring; these 8 plus another 6 offspring; these 14 plus another 6 offspring; then the offspring start to produce so 2 parents, 6 offspring, paired up to produce 18 offspring, plus the other 12 offspring equals 38 mice in just 12 weeks!

Assessment WS 29 WS 30

Use the Unit 3 assessments on WS 29 and WS 30 to check the students' understanding of the content of the Unit. The answers are given below.

Answers

Unit 3 assessment 1

1 The wind carries the pollen, scattering it from one plant to another.

2 Seeds can be scattered by animals, wind, water and explosion.

3 The bigger the egg, the longer it takes to hatch.

4 The egg would take about 21 days to hatch.

5 The egg would take about 16 days to hatch.

Unit 3 assessment 2

6   A-E-B-C-D

7   Human babies need care and attention for a long period after birth. Adult humans live longer to care for them and bring them to maturity.

8   Some from: Both involve male and female, male and female elements combine, new organism produced, both plants and animals grow, both reproduce when mature, both age and die.

Name: _____ Date: _____

WS 29   Unit 3 assessment 1

1 Some flowering plants are wind pollinated. What does this mean?
_____
_____

2 What ways are seeds dispersed? _____
_____

3 The children in Class 5 found some information about birds' eggs.

Bird Egg	Robin	Blackbird	Crow	Raven
Size (mm)	20 x 16	29 x 21	43 x 30	50 x 33
Time to hatch (days)	13	14	19	20

What is the pattern linking the size of these eggs and the time taken to hatch?

4 Tariq found an egg 60 mm long. How long might it take to hatch?
_____

5 Jamila found an egg 35 mm long. How long might it take to hatch?
_____

Name: _____ Date: _____

WS 30   Unit 3 assessment 2

6 These stages in the life cycle of a flowering plant are not in the right order.

A	Growing plant
B	Pollination
C	Dispersal of seed
D	Germination
E	Flower production

Fill in the letters in the correct order to show a plant's complete life cycle.

7 Many adult animals die soon after reproducing. Humans do not. Explain why.
_____
_____

8 Name some ways that the life cycles of plants and animals are alike.
_____
_____
_____

The answer!

Refer back to the introductory question. Students should have enough information to know that all living things need to reproduce to survive as a species, including fish.

And finally...

If you have pets in school, or at home, keep a daily record of what they are doing. Build this into a pet's diary and take photographs to display. Let the students produce a timeline for the animal and a life cycle, as well as graphs of how they have changed in weight and length.

Alternatively, set up a few bulbs in pots and carry out the same exercise with them. Note the daily growth, and weigh them. If you have a digital camera, put the photographs together to 'watch' the plant grow on the computer. Using hyacinths or daffodils is ideal as they produce flowers quickly.

Unit 4: Light

The objectives for this Unit are that students should be able to:

- Understand that there are many sources of light, including the Sun

- Learn that light travels in straight lines and can 'bend'

- Discover that light cannot pass through opaque materials

- Use evidence they have collected to try to explain what they have discovered.

Science background

SB p.37

Light is the visible form of energy. Light is important to us because we receive it with our eyes and interpret it with our brain. Our main source of light is the Sun. Without the Sun's light and heat the Earth would be a frozen wasteland. Stars like our Sun burn with a white light and give out both heat and light. Cooler things that burn, such as fires, give out an orange light, and heat.

Light travels in straight lines; it cannot travel over, under or around objects in its path. Anything that blocks the path of light will make a shadow. We get shadows when light cannot pass through a material. We call such materials 'opaque', e.g. brick, wood, people. A shadow is always cast on the opposite side of the object to the light source.

Materials that allow some light through are called 'translucent', e.g. tissue or tracing paper. Those which allow most of the light to pass through are called 'transparent', e.g. glass, Perspex.

Smooth or shiny surfaces cause light to bounce off them in an ordered way and we see these rays as a reflection. Other surfaces cause the light to bounce off them in a less regular way and do not reflect an image. If light wasn't reflected back to our eyes then we wouldn't be able to see any objects.

The length and directions of shadows change depending on their position relative to the source of light.

Language

Axis	The imaginary line from the North to South Pole around which the Earth spins.
Eclipse	When the shadow of the Moon falls on the Earth or vice versa.
Light beam	A thin line or ray of light.
Light source	Anything that produces light.
Mirror	A shiny surface that reflects light and forms an image.
Opaque	A material that light cannot pass through.
Reflection	Light bouncing back from a surface.
Shadow	The dark shape that falls on a surface when the path of light is blocked.
Translucent	A material that some light passes through.
Transparent	A material that light passes through.

The Words to learn list on page 37 of the *Student Book* can be used to make a classroom display.

Resources

- *Light and Shadows* and *How We See Things* Readers.

- Selection of transparent, translucent and opaque objects including cardboard and white card to make a screen.

- Selection of smooth, reflective surfaces (not just mirrors).

- Computer with light sensor attachment.

- Selection of mirrors.

- Protractors.

- Strong light source – an OHP or desk lamp is ideal.

- Selection of torches.

- A globe, tennis balls, ping pong balls.

- A stick that can be anchored to the ground, e.g. with a rounders base or a pop bottle filled with sand. Protect students' eyes from the sharp top of the stick.

- Measuring tools: tapes, rulers, meter rules.

- A digital camera.

Bright ideas

- Use a light source that can be moved easily. An OHP lamp or an angle-poise desk lamp allow adjustment of the position and angle of the light source.

- Smoothed out aluminium foil makes an inexpensive and acceptable substitute to mirrors. Empty CD cases make surprisingly good reflective surfaces, which have the added advantage of being stable when opened. They can be adjusted to various angles. Some shiny gift wrap can provide mirror-like surfaces.

Knowledge check

- Students should recognize that light is needed in order to see.
- Students should know that there are many sources of light and that the most important of these in the daytime is the Sun.
- Some students believe that the Moon is a primary source of light whereas it is in fact only reflecting the light from the Sun.
- Students can become confused about what a shadow is, sometimes believing that it is a 'reflection' from the Sun rather than an absence of light where light from a source has been blocked.
- Students should be aware that light can be reflected from different objects and materials. Some objects and materials reflect light better than others.

> ⚠ Warn students that they must never look directly at the Sun as they may damage their eyes.

Skills check

Students need to:

- make careful observations and measurements
- collect evidence and decide how good it is
- use their evidence to explain what they found out
- recognize when to repeat measurements
- present results in tables and in line graphs
- identify patterns in data.

Some students will:

- be able to explain that the changes in shadows from the Sun throughout the day arise from the movement of the Earth and that even transparent objects block some light and form shadows.
- be able to explain the difference between shadow formation and reflection in terms of the path of light.

Links to other subjects

Literacy: Reading and following instructions. Writing a play suitable for use with shadow puppets. Introduce folk stories and classics that use ideas of reflection as a motif, e.g. Lewis Carroll's *Through the Looking Glass*.

Numeracy: Measuring and comparing using standard units. Organizing and interpreting simple data in bar graphs and tables. Telling the time – analogue, digital and 24-hour clocks. Measuring angles using a protractor. Reflective symmetry.

ICT: Using a multimedia package to combine text and graphics to make a presentation. Using spreadsheets to record and analyze data. Using a light sensor.

Geography: Using compass directions.

Art: Look at the work of pointillist painters such as Seurat. Look at optical illusions in art, e.g. *The Ambassadors* by Hans Holbein.

Design and technology: Making shadow puppets with moving joints using paper fasteners. Making a sundial.

Let's find out...

The Unit opens with this question:

> *The Radiation Rangers have their base in the shed at the bottom of Abdul's garden. Their rivals, the Laser Lads, have their base in the garden next door. How can the Rangers see the Lads approaching before their garden is invaded?*

Discuss the problem with the students and encourage them to suggest solutions. Perhaps some students may have played with periscopes. Include other contexts where mirrors might be used to 'see around corners', such as on a sharp bend in the road or as a security device in a shop. Note any misconceptions and probe to find the reasoning behind these.

59

Unit 4: Light – Light sources

The objectives for this lesson are that students should be able to:

- Learn how light travels from a source
- Make an annotated drawing of how light travels
- Discover that shadows are caused by light not being able to pass through some objects, such as people
- Find out if light can be measured.

Starter
SB pp.38–39

- Display a photograph of a firework display. *How many of you have seen fireworks or visited a firework display? Do you know that in some countries they have firework displays in the daytime? What do you think they would look like?* Hopefully the students will say that they wouldn't be able to see fireworks very well because the sunlight is too bright. Tell the students that they are going to learn all about where light comes from and how it travels so we can see.

Explain

Where does light come from?

People used to believe that our eyes were active in producing light rays. We see the Sun, the stars, fireworks and car headlights because they are all sources of light. We see the Moon because it reflects the light from the Sun, as do most objects we see in the daytime. Light reflected from them enters our eyes.

The speed of light

Light is the fastest thing in the universe. It travels so quickly that our eyes cannot register its actual movement. We only 'see' what it touches as the light bounces off the objects into our eyes.

How light travels

Light travels in straight lines. It cannot bend around corners or move up, round or over objects in its path. *What is light?* In some ways light is a wave; in others it is a stream of little bundles or particles of energy. Light waves travel about a million times faster than sound waves and as they need no medium to conduct them, they can travel through the vacuum of space. Waves at different frequencies

such as radio waves, microwaves, ultraviolet light and X-rays all radiate from the Sun. While we can't see all of these different sorts of radiation, we can feel the heat from the infrared rays of the Sun and be burned by the ultraviolet rays.

Things to do

Go direct

Light radiates in all directions in straight lines from a light source.

One way to show that light travels in straight lines is to clap some chalkboard rubbers together to produce a fine airborn powder, while over a torch or a projector. The edges of the beam of light should be seen in the dust in the air.

Record

Students should make an annotated drawing of what they have done with arrows showing the direction that the light has travelled from the light source to their eyes.

Support

Build a light box to demonstrate rays of light. Paint the inside of a shoe box black and cut a small hole in the short end and one in the top. Shine a strong torch through the end hole. Put a comb with large, well-defined teeth in front of the torch beam and look at the pattern of light rays inside the box. You should see a pattern of stripes where the light is shining straight through the gaps in the comb and not diffusing.

Extend

Students could try to draw the light rays travelling either down the tube or in the beams to illustrate light travelling in straight lines.

Shadow pictures

Pin black paper to a wall and place a strong light source in front of it. Seat each student in profile between the lamp and paper and draw round the shadow with chalk. Cut out and mount on white paper. Students should notice that the shadow is the same shape as their profile and that it does not show any facial features.

They could try using a range of objects to make up a shadow of an animal or they could use a row of objects to make up a skyline, and then discuss the differences between the shadows and the real thing.

> ⚠ Students should not look directly into any strong source of light.

Record

Make a class display of silhouettes. Can students recognize their friends?

Support

Let students make shadow shapes with their hands to reinforce the idea that their body is blocking some of the light and creating a shadow.

Extend

Students may realize that the position, shape and size of their shadow depends upon their position in relation to the light. Let them experiment moving the light from side to side. What happens to their silhouettes? Can they recognize themselves in profile now?

I wonder...

Most animals do not see in full colour. They can only distinguish between the intensity of light from strong to dim so their view is a bit like a black and white television picture.

Dig deeper

Students have the opportunity to find out more about the colour and brightness of light.

Did you know?

These facts illustrate that light and colour are connected.

Other ideas

Guess what

Shadows relate to the shape of the object that makes them. Let the students play a guessing game with their friends to match the shadow to the object that made it.

Light language

Sailors have used lights to signal messages for centuries. Introduce traffic lights, blue lights on emergency vehicles, flashing lights on aircraft and even the 'on' light on a computer.

Presentation

Make a collage display of sources of light using pictures from magazines and catalogues.

Ask students to pretend they are interior designers and prepare a presentation to suggest different ways of lighting a room.

At home

WS 31

Ask the students to list all the light sources and their uses in their home. Are lights used for illumination, information, warning or entertainment? How many uses can they find? Ask the students to complete WS 31 to consolidate their learning.

Plenary

What can the students remember about where light comes from and how it travels? Create a class mind map on what you have discovered so far.

Unit 4: Light – Blackout blinds

The objectives for this lesson are that students should be able to:

- Identify the best material to block out light

- Plan and carry out a scientific investigation to measure which material would make the best blackout blind

- Develop methods of making their experiment fair

- Make their own stained glass windows to see how light can change colour.

Starter
SB pp.40–41

- Shine a light with a wide beam to demonstrate how a shadow is cast. The shadow has a deep umbra and a lighter penumbra. The penumbra is the area cast by a large light source, where not all the light is blocked. Ask the students to explain what they see. Would the shadow be the same if the light was moved? What if the object were closer to the light? Or the screen further from the object?

The challenge

Read the start of page 40 of the *Student Book* and discuss how Raj's children could find the best material for their father's curtains. Ask the students to do a similar test. Were the children's ideas good or can they think of anything better? Discuss how important it is to test materials we think won't work because that's the way to prove our ideas. Until we can prove that something won't happen, we can never really be certain. Also discuss why the children chose to look at the shadow the material made, so making a link to the amount of light blocked and the darkness of shadow.

What to do

Give groups of students materials to test for opacity. Ask the students to predict what will make the darkest and lightest shadows. Do the students think there are some materials that won't cast any sort of shadow at all?

Ask them to rank their predictions from darkest to lightest.

Heinemann Explore Science

What you need

- a light source
- materials, from transparent to opaque
- a screen
- shade cards (a strip of paper printed in blocks of different shades of grey through to black)
- ideally, a light sensor

What to check

Students will need to do some very careful observing and judging in this experiment – be prepared for animated discussion on just how black this black 'shadow' really is!

Students need to decide which part of the shadow they are going to grade; you might find some materials have darker outlines than centres. *Why is this?*

Support

Reinforce that all conditions apart from the test material should be the same. If the students change the distance of the material from the light source, for example, they will get a different result.

Extend

All students should be able to say that some materials block light and cast dark shadows. Most will be able to rank materials on the basis of opacity and begin to draw conclusions linking the depth of the shadow to how much light the materials let through, although the ranking/ordering of the materials can be subjective unless a light sensor is used to measure the amount of light.

What did you find?
WS 32

Students can use WS 32 to record their results.

Record

Ask the students to order the materials according to their opacity. If their results are inconclusive, use the data as given in the *Student Book*.

The students will need to explain which material they would use for the puppet and why, in terms of blocking the most light and creating the darkest shadow. More able students might also think of other properties of the material too i.e. foil is opaque but not very good material for curtains.

Present

Encourage the students to generalize from their results. They should find that only some (opaque) materials block the light entirely. Some materials (translucent) let some light through and cast a paler shadow. Clear (or transparent) materials let most of the light through and cast very light shadows. You may need to explain all the key words to the students so they can use them in the explanation.

Can you do better?

Would the students approach this investigation differently if they were asked to do it again? If the brightness of the light source was increased then the ranking of the materials shouldn't change but the sharpness and definition of the edges would improve.

Impress on students the importance of making repeated observations and measurements during their investigations to ensure that their results are reliable and reproducible.

Now predict

The test to see whether something is transparent, translucent or opaque is to look through it. If you can see an image clearly through a material then it's transparent, e.g. cling film, glass. If you can't see an object through the material at all then it's opaque, e.g. wood, cardboard, brick. If you can see something of the image but it's not clear, then your material is letting some light through and it is translucent, e.g. frosted glass, tracing paper.

Coloured cellophane lets an image through, just changing the colour of the image, so it is considered to be transparent.

By writing a set of instructions the students are practising a literacy skill.

Other ideas

Stained glass windows

Real stained glass windows are very expensive. Students can make their own versions using black paper and cellophane or coloured tissue paper. They should fold a square of black paper in half to make a triangle then in half again. Let them cut out shapes from each of the three edges and open out the square to reveal a pattern of holes. They stick different coloured cellophane behind the holes. Attach to the classroom windows and admire the coloured light coming through them on a sunny day! *Do coloured pieces of glass cast coloured shadows? Are they darker than other shadows?*

ICT ideas

Let the students use a light sensor to find the shadiest or brightest places in the school. They could make a survey of light and dark places in school and record their results on a spreadsheet. They could make a 'shade map' of the school based on the findings.

At home

Ask the students to draw a picture of part of their home, labelling transparent, translucent and opaque objects. They should include details of where they are and why that material is used, e.g. transparent glass in the window to let light through to see, translucent glass in front door to let some light through but people can't see through it, opaque curtains at the window to block light.

Plenary

Let the students imagine how the umbra and penumbra are formed. If a light source is bigger than the object blocking the light rays, not all the light will be blocked in the outer area – the penumbra.

Unit 4: Light – Changing shadows

The objectives for this lesson are that students should be able to:

- Understand and observe in detail how a shadow is made

- Find out how you can change shadows

- Plan an experiment to test how shadows can be changed

- Display their findings in a suitable way using ICT.

SB pp.42–43   Starter

- Show how a shadow is cast by making shadows on the wall. *What if you could see through the wall? What if you could see the shadow from the other side? What would you see?* If we use a translucent screen to cast the shadows on, we see its shape from the other side. Shadow plays use this to tell a story by casting shadows on a screen that the audience watches from the other side.

- Many students may have seen traditional puppet shadow theatres and understand how the shadows are created. There are many video clips of these puppet shows on the Internet. Although this challenge isn't a traditional puppet theatre, it should allow the students to engage with the process of how they are carried out and some of the tricks used to create movement.

  If you are feeling creative, you could start the session by showing a short film clip, arranging a visit from a local group or even by mocking up a show yourself, hanging a white sheet (dhoti) and using cardboard puppets instead of the traditional leather (thole) puppets. You could also discuss the use of leather, paper or card as 'best' materials for the job.

The challenge

Read the beginning of page 42 in the *Student Book*. Discuss how the children could change the size of their shadow without changing the size of the puppet. *Why do you think one child suggested moving the puppet or the light source?* What effect do the students anticipate this will have?

There is another challenge within this activity to see if the students can observe carefully whether decoration on an object is seen in the shadow.

What to do

Split the students into groups. Give each group an already prepared cardboard shape; a square or rectangle of card stuck onto a blunt-ended stick or ruler will do the job. Students can use their own shadow puppets if you wish but a simple shape is easier to draw round and measure.

What you need

- a screen

- pre-prepared simple shadow puppet shapes

- a strong light source – torch, angle-poise lamp or OHP light

- rulers, measuring sticks or tapes

What to check

The students need to decide on what they are going to measure. They could either measure the distance from the puppet to the screen or from the light source to the puppet. Each will produce a valid graph but the students need to choose one and stick with it.

Support

Discuss how to make the test fair. Only one variable should be changed, i.e. the position of the puppet. Everything else should be the same. To make measuring easier, lay measuring sticks on the floor or table marking off distances of 10 cm until you cover the ground between light and screen. Mark the distance on the outline of the shadow too so as not to confuse the students.

Extend

Students should realize that if you project a shadow on a screen you can change its size by keeping the puppet still and moving the screen closer to or further away from the light source. As you move the screen further away the shadow of the puppet will get bigger.

What did you find?
WS 33

Record

The students can use WS 33 to record their results or if their data is inconclusive, use the children's data given in the *Student Book*.

The students could convert their recorded data into a graph. As you can put the puppet at any distance, the data is continuous so a line graph is more appropriate than a bar chart. Line graphs are demanding, so you could represent the data as a stick graph which is somewhere between a bar and line graph. Less able students can present their results visually by cutting out paper shapes the same size as each of their shadow measurements and sticking them along a metre strip.

Present

Encourage the students to look at their graph and 'tell its story', e.g. 'When the puppet was close to the screen and far away from the light the shadow was small. When it was far away from the screen and close to the light the shadow was much bigger.' Encourage them to use comparative language, e.g. 'bigger', 'biggest', 'smaller', 'smallest', 'closer', 'closest'. Check that their pictures are consistent with their results.

Can you do better?
WS 34

Ask students to review how good their evidence was. How would they tackle the investigation differently if they were starting again?

Show the students the results on WS 34. How many ways can they generalize about changing the size of shadows? *What could the children have done better?* Ask the students to criticize constructively.

Students may also have noticed that as the shadows became smaller, they also became darker and more clearly defined.

Predict

Class 3 need to make sure that the puppets are positioned between the screen and the light

source, with the audience on the other side of the screen. *What materials would you recommend to make a translucent screen? What opaque materials would make good puppets?* The students should recognize that the size of a shadow depends upon the relative positions of the light source, puppet and the screen, and that moving any of these will affect it. The instructions could be recorded in the form of a cartoon strip.

Some students may realize that the brightness of the light source will affect the definition of the shadows. So, in a well-lit room, the contrast between light and dark will not be so clear and the shadows will appear paler. The students could demonstrate the differences and why a dark room is better.

Other ideas

Hand shadows

Invite the students to make hand shadows on a wall using strong light source. Can their friends guess which animal they're making? Draw around the shadows, cut them out and mount them on a display.

At home

Students can use their ideas on opacity to make their own shadow puppets (and scenery). *What will happen to the shadow if you cut holes in the puppet?* Encourage them to write a short play for their puppets. *Does it make any difference if you draw detail on the cut outs?*

Plenary

Remind students of the predictions they made before they started their enquiry – were they correct? Look at their graph. They should notice from their results that the graph is not an exactly straight line; the closer to the screen the slower the change in size related to the distance. If they moved the puppet towards the screen they should see a steep drop in the slope of the graph which gradually becomes more gently sloping.

Unit 4: Light – Sunlight and shadows

The objectives for this lesson are that students should be able to:

- Explore the changes in shadows made by the Sun throughout a day

- Ensure that this is a fair, thorough test

- Record their results accurately in a line graph

- Evaluate how they could have improved their investigation.

SB pp.44–45

Starter

- Explain that you are going to explore the changes in shadows throughout a day. You need to look at the position of the Sun and the size, shape and position of the shadow it makes. Discuss the best way to do this and also to record it.

> ⚠️ Push a cork, a rubber ball or some soft material on the top of the stick to prevent eye injuries if students bend over it. Place the stick in a sunny and sheltered place, well away from any areas where students are likely to knock it over.

The challenge

Read the challenge on page 44 of the *Student Book* and discuss the students' ideas. Does your class agree with Class 5's ideas? If not, why not?

What to do

Decide on how you are going to organize your test. Is everyone going to measure their own stick or pole? Does it matter how long the pole is? Should different groups try different lengths of pole?

What you need

- a sunny day

- a stick and something to anchor it to the ground, or fill a pop bottle with sand

- a measuring stick

- chalk

- ideally, a digital camera

- compass points drawn on the ground

Heinemann Explore Science

What to check

Mark the position of the stick so that if it is accidentally moved then you can replace it exactly. Encourage students to mark and measure the shadows precisely.

Support

Make sure that the students are measuring from the same point each time using the same units. Ideally, use a camera or video to record the changes from one hour to the next. Stand the camera in the same position each time and mark the position.

Extend

Most students should recognize that the position of the Sun in the sky behind the stick affects the length and the direction of the shadow cast. Some may associate the changes with the angle of the light beams hitting the stick. Demonstrate this using a simple model of a pencil held upright in a cotton reel with a torch as a light source.

What did you find?   WS 35

Record

Students can use WS 35 to record their results. This data is continuous so it should be recorded on a line graph. If their results are inconclusive, they could use the data in the *Student Book* instead. The time of day should be on the x-axis and length of shadow on the y-axis.

The students could also mark the shadows on the playground in chalk, so they can photograph this and use it as part of a slide show to make a movie in programmes such as Microsoft Photostory (free to download from the Internet), with a running commentary and labels.

Present

Let the students make a PowerPoint presentation to 'tell the story' of the graph. *When was the shadow shortest or longest? Were increases and decreases in length regular throughout the day?* If they have recorded with a camera or video they could import clips into their presentations.

Can you do better?   WS 36

Ask students how good their evidence was. How could they tackle the investigation in a different way if they started again?

Look at the report Class 5 wrote on WS 36. Discuss this with the students. Have they drawn the same conclusions? Could they have done anything better?

Now predict

Look for an understanding that shadows cast from the Sun change throughout the day. The higher the Sun in the sky, the shorter the shadow. The direction of the shadow and its length will change at different times of day, relative to the position of the Sun in the sky. The position of the Sun determines direction, and the height of the Sun above the horizon determines the length of shadow.

At each recording time, ask students to predict how the shadow will look in one hour.

Other ideas

Make a sunset

Students will have noticed how the colour of the Sun changes at sunset. The colour change to orange at dusk is caused by dust particles in the atmosphere. Show the different colours by shining a torch through a glass of clear water and then adding some milk (to represent dust). The colour of the beam should change from white to yellow/orange.

Control

Using a light sensor program, work out a remote way to switch on the lights in your house when it gets dark.

At home

WS 37

Ask the students to complete WS 37 to consolidate their learning.

Ask the students to look up sunrise and sunset times in a newspaper and calculate the length of the day. What do they notice if they do this every day for a week?

Plenary

Invite the students to imagine that they are television producers. Their cameramen are covering an important football match. They know that they will get good pictures when there is a lot of light but they won't want too much shadow interfering with the pictures. *At what time of day would you recommend that the match is played?* The match has, in fact, been arranged for a 7.00 p.m. kick-off. *What can you do to ensure good pictures?* It is important to make it clear that shadows change in length and direction throughout the day because the Earth is moving rather than the Sun.

Unit 4: Light – How we see things

The objectives for this lesson are that students should be able to:

- Learn how their eyes see things because light bounces off objects

- Discover that their eyes change to allow different amounts of light to enter

- Understand how the eye works

- Distinguish between shiny and dull objects and record their findings.

SB pp.46–47 | Starter

- Display some photographs showing shadows or reflections.

- *What can we see in these pictures that shows us how light behaves?* You might be able to see a reflection, or a shadow. *How can we see things? What do we need in order to see at all?* Use this introductory session as a way to elicit the information that students have already covered earlier in school.

- Write facts that the students know on sticky notes and place them on an appropriate picture or even a mirror in the classroom. As more facts become known students can add these too. Use different coloured sticky notes for 'known' facts and 'guessed' facts.

- Explain that the students are going to learn more about how light interacts in different ways with different materials and surfaces and how this helps us to see different things.

Explain

Scattered sunlight

It is relatively easy for students to identify objects that are light sources and produce their own light. We can understand how light will travel from a source and directly enter our eyes so we can see, but how can we see objects that don't have their own light?

Light bounces off all of the surfaces we can see; if there was no light we wouldn't see the objects. Light bouncing off non-reflective surfaces or rough or dull surfaces behaves a bit like a handful of rubber balls thrown onto a cobbled street. The balls will bounce off the uneven surfaces in all

directions at random, which is just the way light waves bounce off non-reflecting surfaces: they scatter so we can't see images in them.

Windows to the world

We see things because light bounces off an object and into our eyes. The light enters the eye through a hole called the pupil; this is the black part of the eye. A transparent cornea covers the pupil. Light can pass straight through this transparent part. Inside the eye, light passes through a lens, which makes a picture or image on the back of the eye. The back of the eye is called the retina and is covered with special nerve cells. These retinal cells react to the light and send a message to your brain. The image on the retina is in fact upside down but our brains reverse this so we see 'right way up'!

Things to do

Shiny or dull?

This should allow the students to observe the way light is reflected and/or scattered from different surfaces. By drawing just the light path from the source to the object and considering the reflectiveness, the students should be confident that the arrow on the ray is facing the right way.

Light rays

By then drawing the rays of light to show how they have seen the objects, it allows the students to demonstrate if they understand that light *enters* the eye, rather than leaves the eye, which is a common misconception.

Support

Students will need help getting the arrows the right way round and also making sure that the light rays are continuous, i.e. don't have any breaks in them. A ruler should be used to draw the path of the light ray.

Record

The students plan a table to record their results.

Ask students to draw out the path the light rays take as they 'see'.

Bright or dark

When it is dark your pupil 'dilates' or gets bigger, to allow more light to enter, so that you can still see even in low light levels. This is why nocturnal animals not only have large eyes, but very large pupils that allow the animal to see in dim light. As soon as the light levels go up, the pupil contracts to restrict the amount of light and protect the eye. That is why when you go from a dim room to bright light or vice versa, you can't see in the first few seconds as your eyes adjust to the light levels.

Extend

Research nocturnal animals with shining eyes, such as cats. They have reflective retinas – the available light passes through the retina twice.

Record

Either take photographs to show the eyes, or students can draw the eyes before and after with captions.

Dig deeper

Students could find more information about the human eye by looking on the Internet.

Did you know?

The iris, the coloured part of your eye, is a muscular ring that opens and closes the pupil to allow different amounts of light to enter.

We have both rods and cones in the retina. Rods see in black and white. Cones can distinguish colours, but need higher levels of light.

Other ideas

Seeing in the dark

Make a light cave. Use a heavy, dense, black fabric over a desk to completely block out light. Allow the students to experience being in total darkness and describe what they can see. At this stage you could explore what other senses they could use to find their way around. You could provide coloured objects and slowly raise the light levels and ask the students to tell you when the colour becomes obvious, or when the detail of the object is seen. If you have a light sensor, this could produce data on how much light is needed to see in the dark and when we see in colour.

Who's afraid of the dark?

Playing Blind Man's Buff (where one person has a blindfold on and has to catch other people) can be exciting, but also scary. Discussion around the game could revolve around the feelings of fear we have when we can't see. This could be linked to why we are afraid of the dark at night and that scary movies are set in the dark when we think that the 'monsters' will come out! Sensitively discuss why we can be afraid of the dark.

At home

Carry out a survey at home of reflective surfaces and see if there is any pattern between those that are reflective and those that aren't. This should illustrate that a surface that is very smooth and flat will be 'shiny' and therefore more reflective.

Plenary

Focus on 'how we see' rather than reflection. Present diagrams on the board for the students to correct, e.g. lines with gaps in, lines where the arrows are the wrong way round, lines that don't touch the object to show reflection; lines that don't enter the eye.

The students could produce a short checklist to use to ensure that they always get the diagrams correct.

Unit 4: Light – Reflection

The objectives for this lesson are that students should be able to:

- Find out how to change the direction of light
- Discover how mirrors work and what happens when light hits a mirror or reflective surface
- Observe how distorting or bending mirrors can change the reflection
- Draw a record of their findings showing the paths of light rays.

SB pp.48–49   *Starter*

Display a photograph of a skier. Ask the students why the skier is wearing sunglasses. Do they know that skiers need to wear sunscreen too? Do we usually wear sunscreen in the winter? Discuss the environment the skier is in – the landscape is very smooth and white – could this give us a clue to how the sunlight behaves?

Discuss the anomaly of bright sunlight but frozen snow. The light may be bright, but the temperature is too low to melt the snow.

Discuss a fairground hall of mirrors and ask the students to explore how they change with the shape of the mirror. This should illustrate that the reflective surface needs to be flat to be of any real use to us! This could link to the extension activity below with WS 38.

Explain

How mirrors work

Light that bounces off a shiny or smooth surface such as a mirror behaves like a football being kicked against a smooth wall. If you kick the football straight on, it comes directly back at you. If you kick the ball at an angle to the wall, it bounces back but not straight back at you. It bounces at an angle away from you. If you measured the angle from the perpendicular they would be equal. Light behaves in the same way when it hits a mirror or any other reflective surface.

The ray entering the mirror is called the 'incident' ray and the ray leaving the mirror is called the 'reflected' ray. An imaginary line perpendicular to the mirror is called the 'normal'.

Bending light

Many professions use mirrors to see where our eyes can't get to, to see the light being scattered and reflected directly, such as dentists for the backs of our teeth and surgeons to see inside the body. Hairdressers use mirrors to show us the back of our hair so we can feel happy that our appearance is as good as it can be. There are mirrors back to back in changing rooms so we can check our appearance from the back when buying clothes.

Things to do   WS 38   WS 39

Make a mirror

Smooth foil reflects an image. Crumpled foil reflects just as much light, but in many directions. There is no resulting image.

Record

Make a class display of the students' distorting mirrors and complete WS 38.

Support

Ask students to try looking for their reflection in a plastic CD case or the CD itself. Although it's made of transparent material they should be able to see themselves reflected.

Extend

Ask the students if they have ever been to a hall of mirrors and seen their reflection distorted. Ask students to try making a distorting mirror by covering thin card with aluminium foil and bending it gently, or covering a card tube. What is the strangest reflection you can make? Can you make an upside down image? They could look at the bowls and backs of shiny metal spoons.

What can you see?

This activity offers an opportunity to measure the angles of light as they hit the mirror, and draw them, proving that light changes direction when it hits the mirror.

Target practice

These activities need a dark or shaded room. This activity shows that altering the angle of the mirror alters the angle of the torch beam. You can experiment with the different numbers of mirrors and the angles they need to be used at to make this work. You could set this as a challenge for more able pupils.

The angle of reflected light is equal to the angle of incident light, or light falling on an object. By trying to hit the bullseye on a target, the students will model the science behind reflection even if they struggle with the diagrams.

Record

Ask students to draw out the path the light rays take as they bounce off the mirrors. Measure the angles involved and mount these light journeys as a display. Complete WS 39.

Support

Describe the process of reflection and model it to their peers without drawing diagrams.

Extend

Ask students how many mirrors they can introduce into this game. Can you bounce the light off three or even four mirrors and still hit the target? Draw ray diagrams to show this. They could measure the angles, but this is beyond their curriculum at this stage.

I wonder...

Words like 'Police' or 'Ambulance' are reversed because they will be reflected in a driving mirror, the correct way round.

Did you know?

These two facts show some uses of mirrors in space.

Other ideas

Mirror writing

Putting a sheet of carbon paper face up under writing paper produces mirror writing on the carbon paper when you turn it over.

Challenge the students to write a note, in the style of Leonardo Da Vinci, by holding a mirror to one side of their handwriting and trying to make it make sense in the mirror rather than reading it normally.

Presentation

Set up a table with things that use mirrors or reflections to work, such as kaleidoscopes and periscopes, shiny reflective objects, reflective or holographic wrapping papers, metal spoons and mirrors.

At home
WS 40

Ask students to make a list of where mirrors or reflective surfaces are used.

Most televisions have remote control devices. These operate using invisible infrared light rays. Infrared light can bounce off shiny or polished surfaces in the same way that white light does. Ask the students to try switching the channel by bouncing the light from the control off different surfaces in their living room. Can you switch channels from behind the television or by bouncing the ray off the ceiling?

Ask students to complete WS 40.

Plenary

Prepare a series of words made out of horizontally symmetrical capital letters, e.g. B, C, D, E, H, I, K, O and X. You could try BOOK, CHOKE, BOX, or HIKE. Cut the words in half along the centre line horizontally and challenge students to use a mirror to reveal the full word. *Why does this work?* What words are symmetrical around a vertical line?

Unit 4: Light – Unit 4 Review

The objectives for this lesson are that students should be able to:

- Check what they have learned about light in this Unit

- Find out how they are working towards, within and beyond the Grade 5 level.

Students working towards Grade 5 level will:

- Recognize that shadows are similar in shape to the objects forming them.

- Recognize the difference between opaque and transparent materials in terms of their shadows.

- Describe how a shadow from the Sun changes over the course of a day.

- Recognise how to alter the size of a shadow.

- Make observations of changes in shadows.

- Measure length.

In addition, students working within Grade 5 level will:

- Explain that shadows are formed when light from a source is blocked by an opaque object.

- Recognize that shadows are similar in shape to the objects forming them.

- Describe how light travels and that we see things when light enters our eyes.

- Recognize what a reflection is.

- Make predictions about the shadows formed by different objects or materials and make careful observations and measurements of the shadows.

- Measure length and time carefully and accurately.

- Recognize and describe patterns in their data using knowledge and understanding.

Further to this, students working beyond Grade 5 level will also:

- Explain that the changes in shadows from the Sun over the course of a day arise from the movement of the Earth and that even

transparent objects block some light and form shadows.

- Draw diagrams to show how light travels.

- Explain the difference in terms of light travelling between a shadow and a reflection.

- Use their evidence to make detailed explanations of what they found out.

- Indicate whether their data is good enough to answer the question.

Check-up

A still pool of water acts as a smooth reflecting surface because all the light waves bounce off together in the same direction. A choppy sea is less predictable. The light waves are jumbled in the way they bounce off its ever-changing surface and so will be scattered rather than reflected. In this way you can still see the sea but you won't be able to see your reflection in it.

Assessment WS 41 WS 42

Use the Unit 4 assessments on WSs 41 and 42 to check the students' understanding of the content of the Unit. The answers are given opposite.

3

12 midday   9 a.m.

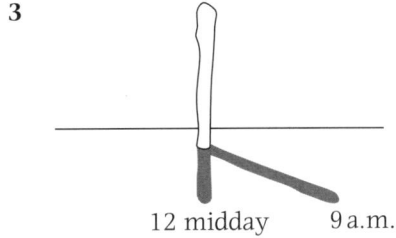

Students should indicate an understanding that the position of the Earth has changed and so the Sun appears to be in a different place. When the Sun is overhead, the shadows are shorter than when the Sun is lower in the sky.

Unit 4 assessment 2

4   Move her hand closer to the torch. ✓

Move the torch closer to her hand. ✓

5   It was shorter at midday than in the early morning (and it had also changed direction).

6   Accept answers that explain that the two surfaces reflect different amounts of light, or that the mirror reflects more light than the paper, which absorbs most of the light.

The answer

Remember the first question? Students should know that the Radiation Rangers could mount mirrors on trees to enable them to 'see around corners'. The images of the Laser Lads approaching would be reflected in the mirrors and then bounced at an angle so the Rangers could see them.

And finally...

Complete the Unit by making an 'outdoor' wall display. Indicate the length and direction of shadows of objects and invite the class to predict what time of day it is. Label each aspect with a question, e.g. *Why is the shadow this shape? What direction is the shadow? Where is the light coming from? Why is this shadow light?* Design Sun protection posters to support this.

Name: _____ Date: _____

WS 42 **Unit 4 assessment 2**

4 Sian shone a light at the wall. Then she put her hand in the light beam. She could see its shadow on the wall. Which two ways could she make the shadow larger? Tick (✓) them.

- Move her hand nearer the wall.
- Move her hand closer to the torch.
- Move the torch further from her hand.
- Move the torch closer to her hand.

5 Anil noticed that his shadow, cast by the Sun, was different in the middle of the day from his shadow in the early morning. How had it changed?

_____

_____

6 'The Sun moves across the sky,' said Anna's little brother. 'It seems to,' said Anna, 'but really . . .'

Explain why the Sun appears to move. Draw a picture to help.

_____

_____

_____

_____

42   Heinemann Explore Science Grade 5

Answers

Unit 4 assessment 1

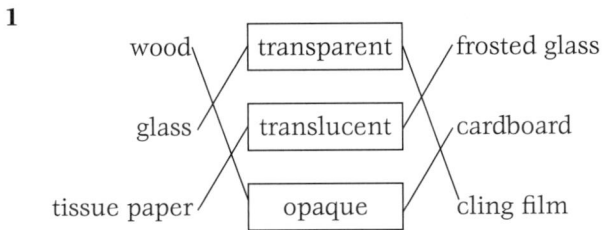

1

wood — transparent — frosted glass

glass — translucent — cardboard

tissue paper — opaque — cling film

2   **a**   The shadow should be attached to the object making it.

The shadows should be the same shape as the object making it.

Shadows do not have any features.

b   The X representing the Sun should be in line in the opposite direction to the shadow cast.

c   Shadows are made when light, travelling in straight lines from a light source, is blocked by an object.

Unit 5: Changing state

The objectives for this Unit are that students should be able to:

- Understand that some materials can exist in different states

- Investigate how water can exist as a solid, a liquid or a gas

- Learn that solids, liquids and gases have different properties

- Recognise that water goes through a cycle.

SB p.51 **Science background**

Materials change with changes in temperature. Ice melts at a relatively low temperature – but it takes a lot of heat to melt iron. Both changes are reversible. The water could freeze to ice again, the iron would cool to solid metal.

Materials can generally exist in three states – solid, liquid, and gas. Solids have their particles crammed together in a fixed shape. Liquids have particles that are far freer to move; pour milk into a bowl, and you expect it to take the shape of the bowl. You'd be very surprised if a pack of butter did the same – except on a very hot day! Gases are free to move. They expand to fill any space available. Balloons can be filled with air – the air doesn't collect down one end of the balloon. The commonest reversible changes we see are water to ice, and water to 'steam' and back again.

Water freezes to ice below 0°C. Most materials contract as they freeze; but frozen water actually takes up more space than liquid. That's why glass bottles break in the freezer. This means that ice is less dense than water, so ice floats. If it didn't, ponds would freeze up from the bottom, and water life would not be able to survive.

What you see condensing on your bathroom window is not steam, but water vapour – water in a liquid state, but vaporized and landing on a cold surface becoming liquid water once more. Real steam – true water gas – is formed at 100°C just above boiling water or at the spout of the kettle.

The molecules of water close to the surface are in constant movement. If they have enough energy, they break free of the water and rise into the sky. If you heat the water, the molecules get excited and break off with far more regularity. The Earth's water cycle starts when the water around us – in

the sea, in rivers, streams, in ponds, plants and in the ground evaporates from the surface and rises into the sky, to form clouds. Plants and trees pull water from the ground and lose it through their leaves – a process known as transpiration.

As the water vapour rises, it cools and condenses, often around tiny dust particles. The smogs of the big cities are caused by water condensing around the waste from fires or car exhausts. Clouds are unstable. As they rise and cool, the water condenses. Droplets run together to form bigger and bigger drops. Finally these drops are so big that they can no longer hang in the air, and they fall as rain. Because this usually happens at quite a height, it is more likely to occur in mountainous or hilly places, or close to them. There are many different types of cloud, classified by their shape and the height they are found at. Some contain minute ice crystals.

If the vapour freezes, it falls as snowflakes. If the water is carried too high, it may freeze. More water gathers round the frozen particle, and it forms a hailstone. Either way, it falls to Earth.

Language

Boil	When a liquid turns to gas.
Boiling temperature	The level of heat needed to change a liquid to a gas.
Change of state	To change from solid to liquid, for example.
Condensation	The process when a gas turns back to a liquid, often seen when water vapour in a bathroom condenses on the cold mirror.
Evaporation	When a liquid turns into a vapour or gas, below its boiling point.
Freeze	To change from liquid to solid when cold.
Gas	A material with weight but no shape. Oxygen gas is needed by all life for respiration.
Liquid	A material that flows into a container to make a flat top.
Melt	To change from solid to liquid when warm.
Particles	Minute pieces of materials.
Solid	A material that keeps its shape.

State	To be a solid, liquid or gas.
Vapour	Drops of liquid in the air.
Water cycle	The closed path of water from cloud to rain to the sea and back to cloud again.

The Words to learn list on page 51 of the *Student Book* can be used to make a classroom display.

Resources

- *Changing State* Reader.
- Several water containers – mugs, lids, saucers, plates.
- Several identical piece of fabric.
- Washing lines.
- Clothes pegs.
- An approved hair dryer or hand fan, possibly – but do **not** use a mains appliance near water!
- Jars with cold water and ice.
- Containers of crushed ice.
- Thermometers or temperature sensors, connected to a computer.
- Timers.
- Clear sandwich bags.
- Sticky tape.
- Measuring cylinders.

Bright ideas

You can demonstrate the whole water cycle by placing a mirror or aluminium tray in the freezer and then holding it over a beaker of hot water that is producing some 'steam'. Watch what happens as the hot water evaporates and the water vapour steams up to condense on the surface of the mirror. You can place a plastic bag over the beaker and see the same thing, as the water vapour condenses on the plastic bag, and runs down the sides into the beaker again.

Knowledge check

- Students should know that materials can be grouped as solids, liquids or gases: that solids have a fixed shape; liquids have the shape of their container, can be poured and have a flat top; and gases have no shape and spread through the space available.

- They will have seen that solids melt to liquids and liquids freeze at low temperatures to solids.

Skills check

Students need to:

- make observations and present them
- identify patterns in their results
- suggest explanations for their observations and conclusions in terms of their scientific understanding.

Some students will:

- give reasons for their predictions using patterns in their data.

Links to other subjects

Literacy:	Reading and following simple instructions, e.g. reading instructions for the evaporation activities.
Numeracy:	Reading scales, e.g. thermometers and volume measures. Organizing and interpreting simple data in bar graphs or line graphs.
ICT:	Using a temperature sensor to measure and record temperature change as ice melts. Using a multi-media package to combine text and graphics to make a presentation.
Geography:	Look at the rain cycle, weather and human settlement; springs, streams and rivers.

Let's find out...

The Unit opens with this question:

'I think it's stopped raining', said five-year-old Anya. Her elder brother Devan was looking at a puddle. It was misty just above its surface. 'It's not stopped for long,' he said. 'The next lot of rain is on the way!'

Was Devan right? How did he know? Why might it rain again later?

Discuss the possibility of further rain. What clues are there?

75

Unit 5: Changing state – Evaporation

The objectives for this lesson are that students should be able to:

- Understand and explain what happens when water evaporates

- Find out that clouds are made up of water vapour

- Measure puddles of water to make a record of changes in the size of the puddle

- Learn more about evaporation when water boils.

SB pp.52–53

Starter

- Complain about the cup of water you keep on your desk. *There was still some water in it yesterday. Today it's gone. The caretaker or janitor must have drunk it last night! Perhaps there is a water phantom around who steals water!* You've noticed that you keep having to water plant pots.

- Take in a solid air freshener stick, a liquid air freshener that evaporates from a container, and an aerosol that sprays air freshener gas into the room. Discuss how each works. *How can they be smelled from far away?* Note that solid air freshener sticks sublimate – they change from solid to gas without a liquid state – there's no need to explain this.

Explain

Solid and liquid

Adventures on and with ice – including the sinking of the Titanic and polar journeys – will remind students of the differences between water in its solid and liquid states.

Students will have had experiences of change of state. They may be curious about how water freezes and increases in volume. The explanation is complex (see Science background) and it's best to explain simply that this is a strange characteristic of water and one or two other rare materials.

Note that water vapour is water in the air below its boiling point. True water gas or steam is water in the air above its boiling point and is invisible.

Evaporation and smells

Evaporation is not a characteristic of water only – other liquids evaporate, often reducing the temperatures of the surface they are on as they do so. (Evaporation needs energy, and evaporating liquids take this energy away.) You feel this when you apply some deodorants or after-shave and they chill your skin.

Other volatile liquids such as nail varnish evaporate. You can smell their particles in the air. Some liquids are harmful, but tincture of iodine and witch hazel, while they must not be taken by mouth, are harmless to the skin. They illustrate that when something evaporates, the liquid is the part that escapes while solid particles are left behind. The activity below illustrates this too.

Things to do

WS 43

Puddle puzzle

A puddle is rather like a very inefficient prison where prisoners are constantly escaping. In order to get away, they have to be at the perimeter of the prison – escaping from the outside surface. The greater the surface area, the more prisoners will escape. And the same is true if the heat in the prison is turned up – the water particles become even more energetic, trying even harder to break away. Every time you use heat to dry something, you are speeding up the rate of escape.

Record

The students could record puddle size, draw changes in the puddle, or take regular photographs with a digital camera. Complete WS 43.

You could run this as a modelling activity or as a role play for the students to explore and demonstrate understanding.

Support

Little is needed. The puddle is clearly getting smaller. However some students may incorrectly conclude that the water is sinking through the surface.

Extend

A measured record of changes in the size of the puddle – say by leaving a metre rule across it and taking measurements every hour – should show, when graphed, that the bigger the puddle, the faster the evaporation (more surface area to escape from). But changes in the environment – more sunshine, for example – are likely to complicate this! Puddles evaporate more slowly when the air is saturated with water – on a misty morning, for example.

Dirty marks

Once the students have grasped the notion of evaporation of a pure liquid this activity should illustrate that in the case of a solution, it is only the pure liquid which evaporates, leaving the solid behind. The students may have met the word 'solution' in everyday language, but have different meanings for this word, such as 'answer' or 'result' as in the case of a solution to a math's question or a riddle.

Record

The students should take images of their dishes to show the solid left behind. They should compare the colour of the solid residue with the colour of the original liquid. Make sure the students consider how they could extend this investigation, to test different solutions, checking if the amount of solid left behind depends on the concentration of the solution, and so on. This is an opportunity to plan and to consider all the factors that need to be taken into account.

Support

Little support is needed in the actual activity, but the interpretation may be harder to explain. A modelling activity linked to the prison reference may help in terms of the bigger, heavier prisoners being unable to escape from the prison.

Dig deeper

Encourage students to explore commercial uses of evaporation. Salt production in Gulf countries is an obvious example, but evaporation of water from a solution to leave the solid behind is also used in the production of sugar, aluminium and other important materials.

I wonder...

Evaporation happens much faster if you put energy into the system. If you heat the water in a kettle, the molecules are excited and break off with far more regularity. The water may 'steam'. Boiling water loses molecules fast and if you are not careful, a kettle can boil dry.

While they are above boiling point, the water molecules are gaseous – water gas. This is the true 'steam'. It's invisible and very, very hot. But the molecules quickly cool and condense as droplets. This is the steam that fills the kitchen or bathroom.

Did you know?

Autumn is a misty season in some countries, but it can be dry, although cold, in Canada – and this results in clear, water vapour-free air and bright colours.

Other ideas

Ask students when they see evaporation and condensation during cooking.

Presentation

Students could pretend to be water particles in a kettle changing from liquid water to water vapour or gas. They could crowd together (water) and then begin to get agitated (warming up), very agitated (boiling) and then escape, one by one (evaporating).

At home

Ask the students to make their own observations of the behaviour of hot and cold water and water vapour next time they bath or shower.

Plenary

Go back to your drink on the table. *So, who did steal it overnight! If it wasn't stolen, is there any way of getting it back?*

Unit 5: Changing state – Investigating evaporation

The objectives for this lesson are that students should be able to:

- Explore how differences in containers change the speed of evaporation
- Plan and carry out a fair test to measure the amount of evaporation in different containers
- Present their findings in appropriate ways
- Come up with a general rule based on their results.

SB pp.54–55 | Starter

- Display a photograph of a rain forest. *Why does it have this name? Why would plants grow fast here?* Even when it is not raining the air feels damp. *Why do you think this is?*
- Revise what the students have learned from the puddle activity. *Why is it that puddles disappear so quickly?* Fill two buckets with water. Take them outside. Pour one on a hard, waterproof surface – an artificial puddle! – and leave the other bucket next to it. *Which will evaporate first? Why?* Be aware of any misconception that the water sinks into the ground. Counter it by creating your puddle in an inflatable paddling pool – without any holes!

The challenge

Read the challenge on page 54 of the *Student Book* with the students and ask them what they think is happening. The shape and size of the pot is important – but so is the shape and size of the plant. A big plant with lots of large leaves is much more likely to lose large quantities of water than a small one! But if you eliminate the plant problem – go just for the container – then what happens to the water?

What to do

This is a great opportunity for playing dumb! Announce that you are going to demonstrate how to tackle this investigation correctly, and then do everything you can to do it unfairly. Expect choruses of correction. Ask the students to answer the three key questions of science:

- What are you going to change?

- What are you going to observe? – or better still, what are you going to measure?
- What are you going to keep the same?

What you need

- several water containers – a mug, a lid, a saucer, a plate
- water
- measuring cylinders

What to check

Where will you put your containers? Why must they all go in the same place? These are key questions for fairness, since differences in temperature will change the speed of evaporation.

For students who are recording water loss over time, it is important to ask them how often they will check the water level. Too frequently will record little or no change, and too rarely will miss the change taking place.

How can you measure the evaporation? This is a challenging question, since what you can measure is not the evaporation, but the water left behind. So the lower the water level, the greater the evaporation. 'Less is more' – something that some students may find difficult to understand.

Support

Some students will need help in understanding why they subtract the remaining water from the original volume to determine the amount of evaporation.

Extend

All students should be able to measure their volumes accurately.

Explain about the meniscus – the curve in water level in a narrow volume measure. Readings should always be taken from the bottom of the meniscus. This can make a difference to the accuracy of the activity.

What did you find? | WS 44

Record

The students should use WS 44 to record the volume of water that evaporated from each container. They can summarize their evidence and produce a graph. If the graph relates container to loss, then it is a bar chart. If it records evaporation at regular intervals, then it is a line graph since the process of evaporation is continuous.

As an alternative, they could use Ajay's data for overall loss, given in the *Student Book*.

Present

Ask each group of students to present their findings. They should include their table of results and charts or graphs. Can they tell the story of the charts/graphs and draw conclusions? Alternatively, the students could present their results as a letter to a company making volatile liquids. Encourage them to explain why it is important to leave the lid on their product – and if they have to open it up, to ensure that the exposed surface area is small.

Can you do better?

WS 45

Show the students Ajay's report on WS 45 and read it together. He has not attempted to explain his prediction although it is correct. *Has he drawn the correct conclusion from the results? Is his explanation sufficient? Could you have done anything better?*

It should be possible to relate the surface area of each container to the speed of evaporation.

For this, students will need to relate a given dimension – say diameter – to evaporation figures. Or they can either estimate the surface area using a grid, or calculate the area using a formula.

Predict

The *Student Book* suggests that evaporation from a container is like aeroplanes taking off from an airport. Ask students to extend the analogy. *What happens if a lid is put on the container? What happens if the lid is only half on – or left loose? Why is it important to keep liquids such as petrol and methylated spirit in closed containers?*

Other ideas

What else evaporates?

Show liquids other than water, e.g. nail varnish and correction fluid as a teacher demonstration.

> ⚠ Volatile fluids are often highly inflammable and must be kept well away from naked flames.

ICT ideas

Use a spreadsheet program to do the simple calculation of loss of water.

If you have one, use a temperature sensor. The students could record changes in temperature and begin to relate these to the speed of water loss. This is a step towards the next investigation.

At home

Ask the students to put two saucers of water in different places in the house. *How long does the water take to evaporate? Which water evaporates first? Why do you think this is?*

Plenary

Take in some domestic paint pots from home. Tell the students you had left some paint without the lid firmly on and now it has got this horrible skin on it. *Where has the skin come from?*

Unit 5: Changing state – Graphing evaporation

The objectives for this lesson are that students should be able to:

- Investigate the factors that affect the speed of evaporation

- Decide how to control the factors to find out which make a difference

- Aim to plan and complete a fair test without help

- Evaluate their findings and scientific methods.

Starter
SB pp.56–57

- Discuss the idea of clothes being hung out to dry, a hairdryer, and puddles drying up. *Can you think of any other examples of evaporation in everyday life?*

- Remind the students about the previous activity. They had found that different factors affected the speed of evaporation.

The challenge

Amani hangs out the washing nearly every day. Some days it drys better and faster than others. She knows when to put the washing out, but can't explain what makes it dry better then. *What makes 'good drying weather'? What sort of day is not a good one for drying?* Encourage the students to agree that a high temperature and a breeze might be good conditions. *But which condition has the most effect, temperature or breeze?* Show them some squares of fabric. Explain that they are going to wet them and hang them up to dry. First, they must decide which factors will make for a fair test of a champion dryer.

What to do

Use sticky notes to consider possible factors that could be changed. Write one on each as the students suggest them.

- Size of fabric square
- Material of fabric square
- Wetness of fabric square
- Where you hang it
- How warm it is
- Whether you blow air at it

Other factors may not be relevant but cannot be dismissed. They include the colour of the fabric square and who is holding the dryer!

Ask the students to decide one factor you will change. For example, if it is whether you blow air at it, then put this sticky note aside and agree that for fairness all the other factors, plus who is holding the dryer, should stay the same.

You may have a problem if the dryer will not blow cold. You are changing two factors, so your test will be whether using a hair dryer makes a difference.

What you need

- several identical pieces of damp fabric
- a washing line
- clothes pegs
- an approved hair dryer or hand fan

⚠️ Do **not** use a mains appliance near water!

- sticky notes

What to check

Decide what will determine that the washing is 'dry'. If you have sensitive, electronic scales, weigh the washing before and after, and agree on a dry weight. A more practical approach is to agree that it will be dry when it feels dry – which might be helped visually by keeping back a dry piece of the same cloth and agreeing that the fabric is dry when the tone matches that of the dry sample.

Support

Most students have a clear idea of fairness, but excitement and competitiveness rule when they think that they can dry their cloth first. Point out that the first one dry is not necessarily the best!

Extend

Challenge their control of factors. Have they thought of every factor that could make a difference to the speed of drying?

What did you find?
WS 46

The students should create their own table to record their results or use WS 46. As an alternative, they could use the data given in the *Student Book*. Encourage them to think about the results in terms of what they know about particles. Heat would make particles of water in the fabric more agitated. A breeze would be likely to knock particles off. You can get confusing results if the day or conditions are very damp. Particles may evaporate, but the same particles may return to the water if the air is already saturated with water. Compare this to crash-landings by aeroplanes!

Record

Amani's first table recorded a change of place. You cannot draw a graph of these results as there is no numerical data. In her second investigation, she recorded the results of a change in temperature. Only if you have two sets of figures, e.g. a change in weight in grams for a change in temperature in degrees, will you be able to create a line graph.

Present

Let each group of students present their findings, perhaps using ICT to make a presentation.

Alternatively, the washing itself provides an engaging presentation. Students could pin explanations to the fabric to show what they did – and what the results were.

Can you do better?

WS 47

Show the students Amani's report on WS 47 and read it together. Although Amani's prediction is correct, the explanation is not. *What could Amani have done better?* Ask the students to criticize the report constructively.

Amani might conclude that there is 'good drying weather'. *What is it?* Get the students to ask their parents what sort of day they would choose to put washing out. Ask them to find out more about drying aids that are used at home. *How does putting the washing on a drying frame, or in the tumble dryer, speed up the drying?*

Predict

Amani tested drying in a place with still air. The fabric still dried, but she found that other factors – how warm they were and whether they were folded or not – made a difference to how fast they dried. Heat makes water molecules move faster and so escape more easily – and unfolding gives a larger surface area for molecules to escape from.

Other ideas

Experiment with washing lines hung in different places. *Do lines near the door or an open window show any differences in drying speed? Why?* Does this experiment explain how and why tumble driers were developed by scientists? What would you look for in a good clothes drier?

At home

Look around the kitchen at home for places where things dry or 'air'. Students might record the sink drainer, the towel rail, an airer, a tumble dryer.

Plenary

Tell a 'washday story' for both times past and a modern family. *How did a family in the past dry the washing? How does a modern family dry its washing? Why is it easier for us to wash and dry our clothes?* Ask students to contribute from their family knowledge.

Unit 5: Changing state – Condensation

The objectives for this lesson are that students should be able to:

- Understand the process of condensation and how it occurs

- Make an annotated, numbered drawing of what happens during condensation

- Find out how to reduce condensation

- Learn whether gases, other than water vapour, condense.

SB pp.58–59

Starter

Ask a student to breathe on a cold mirror. *What is collecting on the mirror and why?* There is water vapour in the student's breath, and this condenses on a cold surface. We can see it best on glass because it clouds the smooth surface.

There are times when a garden is wet, even though it hasn't rained. *Where has the water come from?* It has condensed from the air. We may call this condensed water dew. It collects on many surfaces on a cold morning.

Explain

Bath time

Bathing or showering introduces water particles to the air in the bathroom. It quickly becomes steamy. Water particles falling from the shower are both hot and moving – perfect evaporation conditions! Evaporated water particles meet cold surfaces where they lose their energy and condense. The particles quickly run together, forming droplets and even drops that run down the mirror and drip off.

Faces on the mirror

It is irresistible to want to part these drops and draw on the mirror! But the mirror stays cold, and water droplets continue to condense, obscuring your drawings. Condensed water like this can be very annoying in some rooms – creating the right conditions for fungus to grow. There are various answers – most involve reducing the amount of water in the air in the room – an electric dehumidifier is one; and an extractor fan or water-attracting crystals that you later dry in the oven are others.

Note, by the way, that the everyday use of the word 'condensation' to describe the accumulated water is not strictly accurate. Condensation is the process – not the product!

Forwards and backwards

This process of evaporation and condensation is going on all the time in the bathroom and in other places that get hot, but have cold areas. You can model this with a kettle boiling against a cold window or a baking tray that has been in the freezer.

Things to do

WS 48

Where does the water come from?

Water will condense on the outside of a cold glass jar. This water has come from the atmosphere, and it proves that even on a warm day, the air is still slightly damp. If students breathe on the jar, the water from their lungs and mouth will accumulate on the surface.

Record

Ask students to make an annotated drawing of what they see. Ask them to number the stages – (1) The ice cools the surface of the jar. (2) Water gas from the atmosphere condenses on the cool surface, etc.

Support

It is hard not to believe that the water on the jar has somehow leaked through the glass – but this cannot happen because glass is not porous.

Extend

Ask students to name as many places as they can where they have seen water condensing – mirrors, windows, cold water pipes. What is the general rule that accounts for this phenomenon?

Water in the desert

Make a desert water collector, similar in design to the one on WS 48. Dig a small hole somewhere safe in the school garden, and put a cup in the middle of it at the bottom. Spread a sheet of clean polythene over the hole and weigh down the edges with stones. Finally, put a stone in the centre of the polythene to form it into a shallow cone with its point over the cup. Leave it overnight and take the students to look at it in the morning.

Where has the water come from? Chiefly from the surrounding ground. It has evaporated from the ground and condensed on the surface of the polythene. The cone shape enabled the water to run down into the cup. Don't drink it – although you might not be so choosy in the desert!

> ⚠ Don't forget to fill in the hole to avoid damaged ankles.

Record

Ask students to draw what they did and to annotate their pictures with what is going on. The annotated diagram is a legitimate and valuable way of recording observations in science.

Support

Remind students that the soil absorbs rainwater. That's where the collected water came from.

Extend

Remind the students that they have regained solids from water by evaporation. If losing the water resulted in pure solids, then losing the solids should result in pure water. This process – evaporation followed by condensation – is a way of cleaning water. It is too expensive in energy to use to purify drinking water, but it is used to make other pure liquids.

We call the process distillation – and the product is distilled. Distilled water is pure water, free of any other materials.

I wonder...

Other liquids will condense from vapour. Condensation is an essential part of the production of many liquids. Different grades of oil – petrol, diesel, lubricating oil and tars – can be separated from crude oil because they have different boiling points, and so are condensed out separately.

Dig deeper

The students have the opportunity to find out more about condensation and condensing.

Did you know?

Students may be familiar with stage 'smoke'. What they see is not particles of solids in the air, but particles of liquid. Solid carbon dioxide (dry ice) is made by allowing liquid carbon dioxide to evaporate. This evaporation removes so much heat that the liquid carbon dioxide freezes to a block. When left at room temperature, the solid evaporates and the resulting vapour is heavy and white, so that it billows across the floor in spectacular smoke effects.

Other ideas

Water condenses at night on many surfaces. Ask students to explain why this happens at night and where the water goes as the day warms up.

Presentation

Ask the students to present the story of some explorers, lost in the desert. They find the desert very cold at night, but that is a very good thing because...

At home

WS 49

Ask students to select and fill in the words on the diagram on WS 49.

Plenary

Discuss why the evaporation of water from the Earth, and its eventual condensation to rainwater is so fortunate. What would the Earth be like if the water never went through this vital cleaning process?

Unit 5: Changing state – Investigating boiling and freezing

The objectives for this lesson are that students should be able to:

- Discover that water freezes at (around) 0°C and reaches boiling point at 100°C

- Accurately measure temperature using a thermometer or a temperature sensor

- Present their results in appropriate ways

- Evaluate their evidence and scientific methods.

Starter
SB pp.60–61

- Discuss what students observe when water boils. Look for answers about bubbling, steaming, and even changes in sound; there is a period of quiet before a liquid really boils!

- Safely demonstrate the boiling of water. Take all possible precautions. Keep the students well back, and make them wear eye protection. Point out that water can spit when it boils, and you are being extra careful. Put a thermometer that reads to at least 110°C into the saucepan. Read out the temperature regularly as the water warms up. What do students think the next reading will be? As it reaches boiling point, it will 'stick' at 100°C – or very close. What is special about this temperature? It is called the water's boiling point. If you have a temperature sensor attached to your computer, present the changing temperature on screen.

The challenge

Read the challenge from the *Student Book* on page 60. Ask the students what they think will happen with the ice. It is important to explain that there are practical difficulties in measuring the temperature of water as it freezes. Everybody would need access to a freezer! But remind them of what they already know – water freezes to ice – but ice melts to water. It is very likely that it freezes and melts at the same temperature!

What to do

Use containers of crushed ice. Thermometers and sensors measure the temperature of the surface they touch; if your thermometer is in the space between two cubes it will never measure freezing point. A computer sensor will record the figures or even draw a graph as the ice melts.

What you need

- containers of crushed ice

- thermometers or temperature sensors, connected to a computer

- timers

> ⚠️ In some circumstances, ice can burn. Tell the students not to handle it, especially if it is straight from the freezer.

What to check

There should be a distinct point at which the temperature remains fairly constant. This is the point at which the ice is melting – the freezing point of water. Depending on how pure the water is – and how accurate your thermometer – this should be close to 0°C.

Support

Some students will become restless between taking the readings. An interesting related activity is to draw a single ice cube as it melts. What melts first – edges, sides, or corners?

Extend

How far will the temperature rise? Will the water boil, eventually? Encourage students to think about this. The answer is that the temperature will rise to the temperature of the room – literally, room temperature.

What did you find?
WS 50

Record

The students should create their own table to record the changes in temperature. They can also use WS 50 to summarize their evidence and produce a graph.

As an alternative, they could use the group's data given in the *Student Book*. The data in this enquiry is continuous, so a line graph can be produced that is consistent with the data.

Present

The students could incorporate their graphs and tables into a presentation that explains what happens when the water temperature goes up.

The line graph should show a steady increase in temperature, with a slight pause at freezing point. This is because of the extra energy needed – provided by the warm room – to convert the ice to water at this point.

Can you do better?   WS 51

Look at the investigation on WS 51 and discuss it with the students. *Have they drawn the same conclusions? Could they have done anything better?*

How good is your evidence? What might have affected the results? Inaccurate thermometers, poor contact between thermometers and ice, and taking the thermometers out to read them (they change immediately) will all affect the results.

Students researching Anders Celsius will find that he originally suggested a 1–100 scale for water, but the other way round, so that 0 was boiling point and 100 freezing point. Discuss why this was changed.

Predict

Everything in a room – unless, like a person or a radiator, it has its own energy sources, is at room temperature. This is hard to believe. Students are constantly experiencing this phenomenon, although they may not notice it. Metal objects feel cold to the touch; stone seats are chilly to sit on. By drawing a sketch graph, the students will demonstrate understanding of the temperature 'flattening out' at room temperature.

Polystyrene feels warm; upholstered chairs are warm and comfortable. Some clothes feel 'warm'; and students may be confused because we talk about a 'warm' coat or jumper. What we mean is that it is good at retaining our body heat. Yet different materials may feel hot or cold, relative to our own bodies. This is because they conduct our body heat away from us at different speeds. Metals and stone surfaces, for example, conduct our body heat away very quickly and they feel cold to the touch. Plastics and wood conduct heat away slowly, so they feel warm. Some materials, such as woollen clothing, help us to retain heat so that our hands actually feel warmer when we push them into 'warm' gloves. But they have no heat of their own; the heat is our own body heat; the woollen glove traps air around our hands which we warm with our body heat; our cold hands soon feel warm.

Other ideas   WS 52

Ask students to investigate an ice balloon. Freeze water in a balloon overnight (in a polythene bag in case it bursts!) and float it in a bowl of cold water. Ask the students to observe – and explain – the way it changes with time.

At home

Ask students to find out more – without endangering themselves or the contents – about their fridge and freezer. How does it work? Why does it hum? What is its working temperature? How do foods differ in the fridge and the freezer? Why does ice accumulate inside the freezer? What is 'de-frosting'?

Plenary

Ask students to prepare weather forecasts – including the temperatures in both Celsius and Fahrenheit – for different parts of the world – the Arctic, the Sahara. How are the temperatures different – and what happens to water in these places?

New International Edition

Unit 5: Changing state – The water cycle

The objectives for this lesson are that students should be able to:

- Understand that water is not created, it is part of a cycle

- Explain the water cycle: how water evaporates, becomes clouds, condenses and falls as rain

- Demonstrate the water cycle by making it rain in a bag

- Find out more about the water cycle using the Internet.

SB pp.62–63 | **Starter**

- Display a photograph of rain falling or if you are blessed with a rainy day go outside and watch the rain from under a shelter. Discuss what happens when it rains. *Where does the rain come from? How is it that it can go on raining and not run out of water?*

- Introduce the word 'cycle'. Apart from bikes, students will have heard it in the context of life cycles. Establish that a cycle is circular – unending. The rain cycle, then, is the unending process that 'fills the clouds' ready for the next downfall of rain.

Explain

What a state

The diagram in the *Student Book* should help them to link all the processes they have covered in this chapter, and also in previous ones. This is a scientific diagram of how the states of matter are linked. Stress that this diagram isn't just about water and that is why the solid is not called ice and the gas is not called water vapour or steam. To illustrate this you could write the process on the board and then the water names underneath – water is so special it has its own names for these states. You could then see if there are any other common substances that could be written underneath, e.g. ice cream as the solid, cream as the liquid and then just gas, or frozen orange juice lolly, orange juice and orange juice gas, to help illustrate. Try the same with common gases, e.g. carbon dioxide is known as 'dry ice' when it is frozen, or with other solids we know both as solids and liquids, e.g. candle wax.

You may need to explain the difference between boiling and evaporation, although this is in the Dig deeper section. Boiling is the point at which all the particles of a liquid have enough energy to escape and the point at which there are gas bubbles seen in the liquid. Evaporation is when the liquid particles escape but at a lower temperature to the boiling point. Not all the particles in the liquid have enough energy to escape at this lower temperature. You wouldn't describe a puddle as boiling when the water disappears!

Down came the rain

The molecules of water close to the surface of any area of water, such as the sea, are constantly moving. If they have enough energy, they break free of the water and lift into the sky. This can happen at any time. If you leave a saucer of water on a windowsill, the water will evaporate at room temperature.

Evaporation happens much faster if you put energy into the system. If you heat the water, the molecules get excited and break off with far more regularity. The water may 'steam'. It loses water molecules fast and if you are not careful, it can boil dry. The more energy you put in, the faster the evaporation. Boiling water loses molecules fast.

A handy spin-off of this evaporation process is that the water that rises is clean. It leaves all its impurities behind. There are rings of dissolved material on the saucer.

But the water's journey is far from over. Many possibilities arise. A droplet may join a stream or river. It may soak into the ground, only to emerge somewhere else as a spring or well. It may scarcely touch the Earth, hardly arriving before it evaporates away again. Or it may start a long adventure that includes pushing around a turbine to generate electricity, being boiled to make a cup of tea, passing through one or more humans, or falling through a shower head. It may wash your car, water your garden, boil your vegetables or escape all of these and end up in the sea.

It may be drawn into a plant and combined with oxygen to produce more plant material and so food for animals. Eventually it may find itself back in the sea. And the whole cycle begins again.

Things to do

Rain in a bag

Choose a warm day and set the experiment up an hour or two before you plan to look at it. A 'cloud' of water vapour forms in the bag. Some water condenses on the bag. When a drop has reached a certain size, it precipitates – it drips. It is raining! The whole rain or water cycle is taking place on your windowsill.

Record

Ask students to produce an annotated diagram of what they see.

Support

Little should be needed.

Extend

Ask students to look up 'precipitation'. *How is it related to the water or rain cycle?*

Dig deeper

The students have the opportunity to find out more about the water cycle.

Some of the rain never reaches the sea. It wets the ground, but evaporates back into the air as the ground dries. Plants and animals breathe out water vapour, which floats into the air. Water vapour that has evaporated from the land rises into the sky.

When the vapour meets colder air, it condenses to start a new cloud or it joins existing clouds and makes them heavier with water. The clouds drift through the sky until the water in them falls again as rain.

I wonder…

Elephants wash to keep cool. The water evaporating from their skins cools them in hot conditions.

Did you know?

The facts here are about snow and hail. Remind students that tennis-ball sized hailstones are rare!

Other ideas

WS 53

Ask students to draw a picture of the full water cycle, putting the correct words to explain the processes involved in the right places. Alternatively, use WS 53.

ICT ideas

Ask the students to make a presentation of the water cycle using ICT. Their presentation should show exactly what happens to one droplet of water.

At home

Ask the students to prepare a poem about the water cycle – or just one verse, the rest of the group to take a verse each describing each stage in the water cycle.

Plenary

Discuss times when the water cycle seems out of balance – when heavy rain leads to flooding or lack of rain leads to drought. Where is the water at these times? Why do these natural disasters happen?

Unit 5: Changing state – Unit 5: Review

The objectives for this lesson are that students should be able to:

- Check what they have learned about changing state in this Unit

- Find out how they are working towards, within and beyond the Grade 5 level.

SB p.64

Expectations

Students working towards Grade 5 level will:

- Describe how to change water into ice and steam, and steam into water.

- Recognize the three states of matter and how heating and cooling reverse the changes.

- Describe a few examples where these changes occur, and recognize patterns in data.

- measure temperature and present their data in tables.

In addition, students working within Grade 5 level will:

- Name and describe examples of the main processes associated with water changing state; recognize that these processes can be reversed.

- Recognize that liquids other than water can go through this change of state process.

- Use and explain the terms evaporation and condensation.

- Explain the water cycle in terms of these processes.

- Recognize the boiling and freezing temperatures of water.

- Use patterns in data to make predictions.

- Plan how to carry out a fair test.

- Identify factors to take into account when investigating to ensure a test is fair.

- Make predictions about what will happen.

Further to this, students working beyond Grade 5 level will also:

- Explain how changing conditions affect processes such as evaporation and

condensation, and give reasons for predictions made using patterns in data.

- Clearly distinguish between condensation and evaporation.

- Choose what equipment to use and what evidence to collect.

- Identify results that don't appear to fit a pattern.

- Communicate this clearly.

Check-up

Rain is usually dirtied by the way it collects – running down roofs and gutters. Assuming the lifeboat is way out to sea, the rainwater should be clean. It certainly won't be salty. But remind students that they should not drink rainwater – certainly not rainwater that has stood for a while!

Assessment   WS 54   WS 55

Use the Unit 5 assessments on WSs 54 and 55 to check the students' understanding of the content of the Unit. The answers are given opposite.

Name: _____   Date: _____

WS 54   Unit 5 assessment 1

1 Parminder and Jasminder are investigating evaporation. They put the same amount of water in different-shaped dishes in different places round the house.

a) Why is this not a fair test?

_____

b) What should they do to make it a fair test?

_____

c) How should the girls decide where most evaporation has taken place?

_____

d) Explain what evaporation is.

_____

2 Khaled was puzzled. If all the things in the bathroom are the same temperature, why does water condense on the window and mirror? Tick (✓) the right answer.

a) Water is attracted to glass. ☐

b) Glass conducts heat easily, and water vapour reaching it is cooled very quickly. ☐

c) Water condenses everywhere, but you see it best on mirrors and windows. ☐

54   Heinemann Explore Science Grade 5

Answers

Unit 5 assessment 1

1 a This is not a fair test because they have changed two factors – the containers and the place they put them.

b They should change one factor at a time.

c Most evaporation has taken place from the container with the least water left.

d Evaporation is when a liquid turns into a vapour or gas, below its boiling point.

2 b Glass conducts heat easily, and water vapour reaching it is cooled very quickly.

Unit 5 assessment 2

3 Water evaporates from the surface of the sea.
Water rises to form clouds.
Water in the clouds condenses.
Water falls as rain.
Water flows in streams and rivers to the sea.

4 When a liquid evaporates, it leaves all its impurities behind. It later condenses as a pure material.

5 Water from the pasta will evaporate but condense on the lid and drip back into the saucepan. The pasta will not dry out and burn.

6 In the morning the air was damp, there was no wind or no sunshine in the morning – or perhaps it rained. In the afternoon the air was dry and there was sunshine and/or wind in the afternoon, and it didn't rain.

The answer!

Refer back to the introductory question about whether or not Devan was correct.

Devan was correct as he associated evaporation from the puddle with the formation of clouds and so with further rain.

Name: _____ **Date:** _____

WS 55 Unit 5 assessment 2

3 The rain cycle is jumbled. Match each sentence to a number to put it in the right order.

Water evaporates from the surface of the sea. [1]
Water falls as rain. [2]
Water in the clouds condenses. [3]
Water rises to form clouds. [4]
Water flows in streams and rivers to the sea. [5]

4 Explain how evaporation can make liquids pure.

5 Safia's mother put a lid on the pasta she was cooking in a saucepan. 'Even if I forget it, it will stay moist,' she said. How did she know?

6 Salim pegged out his washing on a cloudy morning but it was still wet at midday. In the afternoon the wind blew and the Sun came out. It dried quickly. Explain why this happened.

Unit 5: Changing state 55

And finally...

Some things grow in clouds! Cloud forests are unique ecosystems in tropical mountain areas, mostly in South America. Because the forests are continually in cloud, the air is completely saturated with water, which is constantly streaming from the trees. Because it is so wet, the trees are covered in epiphytes – plants that grow on other plants – such as orchids, mosses and ferns. Some of the huge tree fern types date from the time of the dinosaurs.

Compare the growth of cloud forest air plants with flowering plants in the classroom. Both have the same needs. Grow plants from avocado seeds by balancing the avocado nut in a bottle top with part of it in water.

Find out more about the endangered plants and animals of the cloud forest – birds with amazing names such as the three-wattled bellbird, emerald toucanet and the bare-necked umbrella bird, the tanager and antpitta; also, mammals such as the spectacled bear, howler monkeys and olingos.

89

Unit 6: The Earth and beyond

The objectives for this Unit are that students should be able to:

- Understand that the Earth, Moon and Sun are part of the solar system

- Make careful observations and measurements throughout their investigations

- Describe seasonal change and explain its cause

- Name some scientists who made discoveries about the solar system and state what these discoveries were.

SB p.65

Science background

Since the beginning of time, humans have been fascinated by the movement of the stars and the planets. People believed that their destinies were controlled by the heavens and the ancient astronomers who first observed and charted these celestial movements were powerful men. Science now tells us that far from being home to the gods, the Sun and stars are just big balls of gas and the moons and planets are chunks of space rock.

Since ancient times astronomers have known of the eight major planets in our solar system, the four terrestrial planets: Mercury, Venus, Earth and Mars and the four giant gas planets: Jupiter, Saturn, Neptune and Uranus. Their movements relative to the stars have been tracked and predicted accurately for centuries, especially by the Egyptian astronomer Ptolemy and by others before and since. In 1930 Pluto was discovered and initially classified as a planet, the outermost one of our solar system. However, Pluto was always anomalous, being very small (smaller than the Moon), having a huge moon of its own (Charon, about half the size of Pluto) and having an irregular orbit. Following the discovery of other bodies in our solar system of a size similar to Pluto, especially Eris in 2005 and then Ceres, it was decided in 2006 to create a new class of planetary bodies, called dwarf planets. Pluto, Eris and Ceres are all now classified as dwarf planets, not as planets. So the number of true planets is again eight.

Much of the content of this Unit will have been touched on before in other contexts in science, maths or geography. You may like to revise some of the work done in the Unit Light before

beginning. This Unit concentrates on how the periodic changes of the Moon and the Sun follow predictable patterns and how the movement of the Earth give us our days, nights, seasons and years.

The Earth orbits around the Sun in a regular pattern. The Earth also spins around its axis. This spinning causes day and night. At any one point in time, half of the Earth is in light and half in darkness. Because of this movement, the Sun appears to move across the sky from East to West.

During the day, the length and position of shadows cast in sunlight change and we can use these changes to tell the time of day.

Language

Astronomer	A scientist who studies the stars, planets and other objects in space.
Axis	An imaginary line through the poles of a planet.
Constellation	A group of stars that form an imaginary pattern in the sky.
Moon	A natural satellite that orbits a planet.
Orbit	The curved path around a planet or Sun.
Phase	The apparent change of shape of the Earth's Moon.
Planet	A large object orbiting a star and reflecting the light from that star.
Satellite	An object that orbits a planet.
Space	Everywhere beyond the Earth's atmosphere.
Sphere	A ball-shaped object.
Star	A massive ball of burning gases in space which gives off heat and light.
Sunrise	The time the Sun can first be seen above the horizon.
Sunset	The time the Sun drops beneath the horizon.
Waxing	The phases of the Moon where its size appears to increase.
Waning	The phases of the Moon where its size appears to decrease.

The Words to learn list on page 65 of the *Student Book* can be used to make a classroom display.

Resources

- *Earth, Sun and Moon* Reader.
- A selection of balls and spheres.
- A globe.
- Torches or strong light sources.
- Range of lenses, both convex and concave.
- Newton metres.
- A selection of secondary sources and books.

Bright ideas

- Plan a visit to a planetarium or observatory.
- Students will be asked to look at sunrise and sunset times. Start looking out for these in the newspaper and make a collection throughout the year – you don't need times for every day but real data is always more meaningful.
- Collect records of the phases of the Moon from newspapers and enlarge them for display.

Knowledge check

- Students may have their own ideas about space. They may believe, for example, that the Sun moves and the Earth stands still. We even talk about the Sun 'rising' and 'going down' as if it were the Sun that was actively moving. Although the idea was questioned by Copernicus and later disproved by Galileo, the movement of the Sun was accepted science until the fifteenth century.
- Other commonly held ideas include the theory that the Moon covers the Sun at night and that the shadow of the Earth is what causes the apparent change in the shape of the Moon.
- Some students might believe that there is no gravity on the Moon or that things float on the Moon because there is no air pressing them down.
- Students often think that we have summer because we move closer to the Sun.

> ⚠️ Warn students that they must never look directly at the Sun as it can damage their eyes.

Skills check

Students need to:

- make careful observations and measurements, particularly of forces

- collect evidence and decide how good it is
- realize when to use secondary sources
- use their evidence to explain their findings
- understand that the answers to some experimental questions can only be inferred from indirect evidence
- generalize from their results.

Some students will:

- explain that the changes in the appearance of the Moon over a period of 28 days arise from the Moon orbiting the Earth once every 28 days
- independently represent times of sunrise and sunset in graphs.

Links to other subjects

Literacy:	Reading myths and legends about the Earth, Sun and Moon, e.g. Greek myths.
Numeracy:	Measuring and comparing using standard and non-standard units.
Music:	Gustav Holst's *The Planet's Suite* is appropriate.
ICT:	Using multi-media to combine text and graphics to make a presentation.
Geography:	Studying seasonal temperature changes, tides and the Moon, time zones, the formation of landscape features such as craters.
History:	The life of scientists who have studied the stars and the solar system.

Let's find out...

The Unit opens with this question:

Vijay and Mohan were camping in their back garden. They lay on the ground looking up at the stars in the night sky. Vijay noticed that a bright star had disappeared behind the wall of their house. Why had that happened?

Have any students experienced a really starry night? In urban areas, stars are difficult to see because of the amount of light pollution. *What is a star? Do you know the names of any? Do you think the stars are moving or maybe it's something else? What do you think might be happening, based on our experience of the Earth and our own star, the Sun?*

91

Unit 6: The Earth and beyond – Our solar system

The objectives for this lesson are that students should be able to:

- Discover the relative sizes and distances between the Earth, Sun and Moon

- Make a scale model of the solar system as a class and be able to label each of the planets

- Understand that it can be difficult to collect evidence to test scientific ideas

- Find out more about the planets and decide which is their favourite one.

SB pp.66–67

Starter

- Display photographs of the solar system and various planets.

- Play some suitable space music to set the scene – the opening of Star Trek or Star Wars, for example.

- What do we know about space? Collect students' ideas by playing a carousel game. Divide the students into teams. Give each team two minutes to write down words, phrases or facts connected with space. Each team should use a different coloured pen to differentiate their contributions into 'known' and 'thought'. After two minutes they pass their paper to another team and receive a paper from a third team. In the next two minutes they must write some more facts but not repeat anything that the other team has written. Continue until every team has seen every other team's ideas. In this way, a lot of information will circulate quickly around the class and the students will be able to share ideas. Play some fast music to mark the time and encourage a sense of urgency.

Explain

Celestial spheres

If we look at our world standing on the ground it does look flat – apart from the odd hill and valley! We can't easily see the curvature of the Earth because we are so small and the Earth is so big. We now know that the Earth is one of the planets orbiting the Sun. The planets are approximately spherical because of the way their gravity holds them together. Some planets have satellites or moons orbiting them and these, together with the asteroids, comets and space dust make up what we call our solar system.

When you look closely at the images of the Earth and Moon, there should be some evidence that they are spheres rather than 2 dimensional circles. This is in the form of shadows – if the object was flat, then there wouldn't be a shadow appearing about three-quarters of the way round the shape! You can model this with footballs and a torch.

Most ancient cultures, including Greece, India and China and the aboriginal cultures of the Americas, believed the Earth was flat.

Measuring the Earth

It was only when rockets first photographed the Earth from space in the 1950s that scientists had final proof that our planet was a sphere. Before then scientists were able to draw on indirect evidence suggesting that the Earth was spherical.

Ancient scientists used their observations of the Sun to estimate the size of the Earth – and they were pretty accurate. You can use a simple model to show the curvature of the Earth and the effect that they first noticed, of ships' masts appearing over the horizon first, rather than the whole ship at once.

Other evidence includes the fact that the patterns of stars change as you move either to the north or the south; some constellations appear to disappear behind the horizon while others come into view.

Things to do

How big? How far?

All of these activities are designed to build knowledge of the solar system and the relative sizes of and distances between the planets.

Record

As a class, make a scale model of the solar system and string it across the classroom. The scale is hard to achieve with the size of the planets in relation to the Sun, so the Sun could be left out. Invent your own mnemonic for remembering the names and order of the planets, e.g. **M**y **V**ery **E**ducated **M**other **J**ust **S**erved **U**s **N**oodles.

Support

The vastness and scale of the solar system is difficult for students to grasp. If the Sun were the size of a large beach ball, for example, then the Earth would be about the size of a pea. If you have a large playground or yard ask individual students to pace out the distances of each planet from the Sun:

Planet	Distance from Sun in millions of km	Distance from Sun represented as students paces
Mercury	58	6
Venus	108	10
Earth	152	15
Mars	228	22
Jupiter	778	78
Saturn	1427	140
Uranus	2870	290
Neptune	4497	450

Extend

Let the students work out their own scale of measurements to represent the relative sizes and distances between the planets.

Dig deeper

Ask students to research the newly classified dwarf planets. They should find out what the definition of a dwarf planet is, how many planetary bodies are currently classified as dwarf planets and where their orbits are. They could produce a chart to present to the class to show their findings.

Did you know?

Scientists do not know where or even if the Universe ends and even the most powerful telescopes can only see a tiny fraction of what lies beyond our Earth. Some of the stars we see are so far away that their light takes immense lengths of time to reach us. For example, the stars in the constellation of Orion are 110 light years away. The Pole Star, Polaris, is even further away at 680 light years. The light from this star started its travels in the Middle Ages.

I wonder...

At the speed of light the journey to the Sun would take around eight minutes. If you were to drive there at 70 mph it would take you over 200 years.

Other ideas...

Flat Earth

Ask the students to imagine that they are scientists trying to persuade the members of the Flat Earth Society that their ideas are incorrect. *How would you persuade them to change their minds? What evidence would you give them?*

Name that planet!

The Greeks discovered the first five of the planets in our solar system and named them after their gods. The final two planets were discovered after the advent of telescopes and are also named after gods. Earth is the odd one out! Invite students to find out about the gods the planets were named after.

ICT ideas

Students could use PowerPoint to prepare a presentation on one of the planets in our solar system.

Presentation

Ask each student to write their Universal address. This should include their house and street, town and county, country, continent, hemisphere, planet, solar system and galaxy. What might the address of an alien penfriend be?

At home   WS 56

Ask students to look at a television guide for a week and count and list the television programmes that are to do with space or space exploration. Why do you think these programmes are so popular?

Ask the student to complete WS 56 as homework.

Plenary

Tell the students about a programme called SETI (the Search for Extra Terrestrial Intelligence). It uses idle computer time to analyze data received from radio telescopes searching space for messages from aliens – so far there haven't been any.

Unit 6: The Earth and beyond – The Earth, Sun and Moon

The objectives for this lesson are that students should be able to:

- Understand that the Sun is our nearest star and the centre of our solar system

- Learn about what gravity is and why we need it

- Find out how to measure forces such as gravity

- Research ancient astronomers and what they thought about the solar system.

SB pp.68–69

Starter

- If you have an orrery, use this to show how the Earth and Moon orbit the Sun. An orrery is a tabletop model of the solar system. Some are motorized. Use it to demonstrate how a shadow is cast on the Earth when the Moon moves between the Sun and Earth as an eclipse, as well as how the Earth and Moon are lit by the Sun. Revisit the idea that we see them because the Sun's light reflects off them into our eyes.

Explain

The Earth

Although there is speculation that there are other solar systems that may have life, we may never know as the universe is so vast. We need to celebrate the uniqueness of the Earth and look after it! The gravity the Earth has not only helps keep us on the Earth, but also the water we need and the atmosphere that allows us to breathe. Many other planets have atmospheres, but some are sulphurous and therefore poisonous for us to breathe, and some planets have either no gravity, or so much that we would be crushed into a pinpoint of matter if we landed there.

Our own star

Explain that the Sun is our nearest star and that it gives out both light and heat. On a sunny day we can see the light and feel the warmth on our skin. The Sun burns, turning hydrogen into helium. As it burns it gives off energy in the form of heat and light. The Sun's surface has a temperature of around 6000°C and glows white hot. The Sun gives out many types of radiation, some of which are filtered out in the atmosphere but some get

through and can do us damage – ozone gas in the atmosphere, for example, filters out harmful ultraviolet rays which can harm our skin.

The Sun is the star at the centre of our solar system. It looks bigger and brighter than other stars only because it is close to us. The Sun is only one of a hundred thousand million stars that make up our galaxy. The Milky Way, our galaxy, is only one of billions in the universe.

Before Copernicus and Galileo, scientists had believed that the Earth was the centre, not just of the solar system, but of the universe. Ancient Indian cultures believed that the Earth was held in place by elephants standing on the back of a giant tortoise, and the ancient Greeks had their idea of the planetary system arranged with the Sun, Moon and planets circling the Earth. Now we understand that the Earth is one of the planets which orbit around the Sun.

What is the Moon?

The Moon is a satellite of the Earth and it orbits the planet at a distance of between 348 000 km and 398 000 km. Apollo astronauts brought samples of Moon rock back to Earth which told us that the Moon was formed about 4–6 billion years ago. The surface is covered with mountains, dark plains and craters formed after the impact of meteors. Stepping onto the Moon, astronauts found it was covered in crunchy dust. There is no atmosphere on the Moon and nothing can live there. Astronauts had to take their own oxygen supplies. If you looked up into the Moon's sky it would always be black as there is no air or vapour to scatter the rays of the Sun.

Things to do

Gravity

There are many ways to lose weight, and travelling to the Moon is one of them – but only because gravity on the Moon is so much less than that of the Earth.

Because the Moon is much smaller than the Earth, its gravity is much less – one-sixth of the pull. In deep space there is little gravitational pull and astronauts become weightless. They float around inside their spacecraft. At night, they have to strap themselves into bed to stop from floating away.

This activity offers students an opportunity to practise their measuring skills using forcemetres or Newtonmetres.

The students will need to decide on a table design (2 columns – weight on Earth (in N) and weight on the Moon (in N)). By providing a range of measuring devices, e.g. rulers, balances, Newton meters of difference scales etc., you can review whether the students can choose the best piece of apparatus for the task in hand.

Support

To help clarify, discuss what each piece of measuring equipment is for. Students may need some help with the calculation of the weight on the Moon, dividing by 6.

Extend

Some students may be able to carry out a similar task if you provide the gravitational pull of other planets, so extending their table.

Earth	= 10 N	Jupiter	= 23.6 N
Moon	= 1.7 N	Saturn	= 9.2 N
Mercury	= 9 N	Uranus	= 8.9 N
Venus	= 3.8 N	Neptune	= 11.3 N
Mars	= 3.8 N		

Alternatively they could describe which Olympic records would be easy or hard to break if we held the competition on the Moon. Which planet would you want to do the sport on?

I wonder...

The size of the Moon is approximately one-sixth of the Earth – so is its gravity. Generally the size of a planet is proportional to its gravitational pull.

Dig deeper

Students find out more about our solar system and Nicolaus Copernicus's discoveries. They can also research how the Earth makes its orbit around the Sun.

Did you know?

Many ancient cultures venerated the Sun as a god. The Mayan civilization constructed solar calendars and were able to predict events like solar eclipses many centuries into the future.

The Japanese word for Japan (pronounced Nihon or Nippon) is made up of two Kanji characters: The first means Sun or day, the second means origin or root.

Other ideas...

Life in space

Ask students to use their knowledge of the Moon to design a Moon base where scientists could live and work. *What would they need? How would they get water? What about breathing? How will they protect themselves from the searing heat of the Sun? How will they get rid of waste?*

Other planets in our solar system

Invite the students to find out which planets have moons and see if they can name them. Add them to the database of planets and the solar system display.

ICT ideas

The surface temperature of the Moon varies greatly between 110°C when the light of the Sun is on it and −185°C when it is in shadow. The space missions landed on the lit side of the Moon. If you have one, use a temperature sensor to find which material would keep the astronauts coolest by reflecting the heat of the Sun. Try using white, black and shiny fabrics and use a lamp as your heat source. Cover your sensor in the fabric and plot the temperatures on a graph.

Presentation

What do you think it would be like to walk on the Moon? Students could present a drama of performing Olympic sports on the Moon.

At home

Find out what ancient civilizations thought about the Moon and the Sun.

Plenary

Add the gravity to the scale model display of the planets and draw creatures that may live there, e.g. on Mercury they won't need to be very strong as the gravity is so light, but creatures from Jupiter would have very thick, strong bones and would probably be very short.

95

Unit 6: The Earth and beyond – Our turning Earth

The objectives for this lesson are that students should be able to:

- Understand that it is night and day at the same time in different parts of the world

- Model how the Earth spins on its axis

- Explore whether it is the Sun or the Earth that moves

- Plan and carry out an investigation on how the Sun moves using a sundial.

SB pp.70–71 — Starter

- At any time, half of the world is illuminated and half is in darkness. Look at the illustration on page 70 of the *Student Book*. Explain that Sahem's torch represents the Sun. Ask the students to explain what it would be like on both sides of the globe.

- Remind the students that light travels in straight lines and that shadows are made when light is blocked. *Does that help to explain the picture?*

- *Half the world isn't dark all the time, though, is it? Can you explain why?*

Your challenge

Read the challenge on page 70 and discuss why Sahem should wait until night-time to phone his dad.

What to do

- Use a globe and a strong light source (an OHP light is ideal) to demonstrate what Minah shows Sahem. Darken the classroom to make it most effective. Students should see that the half of the planet facing the Sun is lit up while the other half is in darkness. As the Earth turns, the lit surface moves into darkness and the dark half moves into light.

What you need

- a spinning globe

- a torch or strong light source

- card

- Blu-tack or sticky tape

Heinemann Explore Science

What to check — WS 57

Support

Explain that the Sun never moves; it is the Earth that moves. Also, point out that the Earth is tilted through 23° on its axis so that when they draw examples of night and day they should notice that the boundary line cuts across the axis rather than follows it.

Extend

A Moon in a shoebox helps us to explain why a shadow changes the apparent shape of the Moon. Students can use WS 57 for this activity. Paint the inside black to represent space. Put a small hole in one end through which to shine a torch beam to represent the Sun. Mount a ping-pong ball on a pencil pushed through the lid – this is the Moon. Cut three viewing holes in the long side of the box. Looking through each viewing hole shows a different angle on the Moon.

What did you find?

Record

Students should recognize that the Sun rises from the east each day and continues to rise in an arc until it reaches its highest point around midday. It then sets in a westerly direction.

If you have a south facing, sunny window the students could repeat Sahem's investigation with the stickers showing the position of the Sun over the course of a day.

You might also want to repeat the shadow stick investigation from the Unit 'Light'. This is a useful exercise in itself as it revises how shadows are formed and that the source of light (the Sun) is always behind the shadow. This means that as the Earth changes position relative to the position of the Sun, the Sun appears to us to be in a different place and so the length and direction of the shadows change.

Alternatively, demonstrate this quite simply using a torch and a pencil stuck in a cotton reel or in a piece of plasticine.

Present

Students should present their ideas to the rest of the class or to a younger class of students, perhaps using ICT.

Can you do better?
WS 58

How well do these models and presentation explain how the Earth moves? If they had to start again would they do anything differently?

Students use WS 58 to write to their penfriend (real or imaginary), filling in the blanks to show their understanding of why we have night and day.

Predict

The Sun rises in the east each day and sets in the west. This is because the Earth is spinning in an anticlockwise direction and so we see the Sun on the eastern side as we come into the light.

However, it does not rise or set at the same time every day. This is because the Earth moves around the Sun and the Earth's axis is tilted. For part of the year, for example, the northern hemisphere is tilted towards the Sun and this gives longer days; in the winter the days will be shorter. If the Earth's axis were not tilted we would have exactly 12 hour-long days and no seasons.

By drawing a sketch this will help show if the students understand.

Other ideas

Make a sundial

People have used the movement of the Earth to measure time for centuries. Use the fact that the Sun casts different shadows at different times of the day to construct a sundial. You'll need a circle of card on which to write your calibrations and a gnomon, or shadow stick, that will cast the shadows. Using a slanted gnomon produces the best results – particularly if the angle of slant is the same as the angle of the latitude where it is being used. Use a compass to line up your sundial in a north–south direction on a sunny day. Ask students to visit it every hour to mark the time on your dial.

The term 'gnomon' comes from the Greek, meaning 'know' and it was called this because it 'knew' the time!

At home
WS 59

Have you ever tried counting the chimes of a clock up to twelve? How often have you lost count? Ask the students to imagine what it would be like if we had to count up to 24! In the early fifteenth century people changed their clocks from chiming 24 times to the double 12-hour system that we use today. Sometimes, however, we use the 24-hour clock system – particularly when we have to distinguish between afternoon and morning. Ask students to collect as many examples as they can of times written using the 24-hour clock. These might include railway timetables or television listings. How many more can they think of? *Why is this system useful?*

Ask students to complete WS 59 as homework.

Plenary

Play a game using a globe. Give the students the name of a country where it is noon and ask them to find the place on the globe where it would be the middle of the night, e.g. UAE/Canada, UK/New Zealand, Mexico/India, Japan/Brazil, etc.

Unit 6: The Earth and beyond – Astronomers

The objectives for this lesson are that students should be able to:

- Learn that many scientists have contributed to how we understand the solar system

- Observe how scientists use careful observations and measurements

- Understand that scientists are still finding out new things about the universe

- Produce a table showing names for the Sun, Moon and stars in other cultures.

SB pp.72–73   **Starter**

Start with an image of the world as a flat disc being carried on the back of elephants and ask how this image might have been arrived at, as a model for the Earth, and Sun and Moon moving together. The students could present explanations.

Read some of the stories that ancient peoples have used to explain the solar system, e.g. 'How the Coyote arranged the Sky' from Native America, or 'Anansi the spider' – A tale from the Ashanti.

Explain

Ancient Egyptians

Many ancient cultures had myths about the role of the Sun and many people believed that the Sun was a god. The ancient Aztec, Mayan and Inca civilizations all worshipped the Sun as a god.

The Sun is the star at the centre of our solar system. It looks bigger and brighter than other stars only because it is close to us. The Sun is only one of a hundred thousand million stars that make up our galaxy. The Milky Way, our galaxy, is only one of billions in the universe.

Then came the Greeks

Aristotle believed that the Earth was at the centre of the universe (as the ancients called the solar system). This theory was in conflict with Aristarchus of Samos who proposed a helio-centric or Sun-centred universe.

Further developments

Although Copernicus and Galileo are credited with discovering how the solar system works, there are numerous contributions from across the world to the idea that the Sun was at the centre of our solar system. Copernicus used many tables and figures from observations made by Muslim astronomers.

Things to do

Discoveries

Nicolaus Copernicus was an astronomer who trained as a priest but set out to make the ideas of his predecessors more coherent. He first put forward the idea that the Sun was at the centre of our solar system rather than the Earth. He used a range of mathematics to explain scientifically, why the Sun was at the centre of the solar system with the planets arranged around it. His model was correct by today's standards, but it was a shift from a completely different model.

Galileo Galilei or Galileo, as he is more often known, was an Italian scientist who made many contributions to astronomy and other areas of science. He discovered the phases of Venus, sunspots and four of the major satellites orbiting Jupiter are named Galilean Moons after him.

Other important scientists who made discoveries about our solar system include Ptolemy, Aristotle, Aryobhata, Tusi and Plato.

Record

Students could record information from their research in the form of a fact card on each scientist. They could extend this to Arab scientists too.

Support

Provide some students with fact card prompts such as: Name of scientist; Place of birth; Most famous works; Important discoveries; etc.

Extend

They could extend this to other scientists too.

Telescopes

In this activity students will be able to experiment with making objects appear bigger, by combining lenses. By using a range of strengths of lenses they can alter the 'power' of the magnification. They may also find how the appearance changes if they use two convex lenses, as opposed to using a convex and a concave lens.

Record

Draw a diagram with labels of the best telescope they made that magnified the most.

Support

Reduce the number of lenses available and model how these can be used, either by changing one at a time, or by moving the lenses further apart.

Extend

Students may find it beneficial to draw a light ray diagram of how they see these images.

I wonder...

This should encourage the students to consider that we don't know everything yet and that scientists are still finding out new things about the universe and naming new planets and stars.

Dig deeper

Claudius Ptolemy lived in Alexandria, Egypt, just after Artistotle, and like Aristotle, believed that the Earth was 'still' because if it moved we would feel 'great winds' as it moved. Although, to back up his belief, he had to alter the evidence to fit his ideas. True scientists alter their ideas to fit the evidence.

The Ptolemaic order of spheres from Earth outward is:

1 Moon	5 Mars
2 Mercury	6 Jupiter
3 Venus	7 Saturn
4 Sun	8 Fixed Stars

Alhazen Ibn al-Haytham, also known as Alhazen, was one of the first astronomers to challenge the Ptolemaic model of the universe in the 11th century. During this time, many other astronomers took up the challenge that Alhazen posed and started to make up their own models

of the solar system. Alhazen did not throw out the Ptolemaic system completely, but cast doubts about some of its elements as it was not based on strong evidence, i.e. using a scientific method but sometimes making the evidence fit the theory rather than the other way round!

Did you know?

This fact helps to bring more modern scientists into the story of the discovery of how the universe works. Without gravity, not only would we not stay on the Earth, but the planets wouldn't orbit the Sun, and the Moon wouldn't orbit the Earth.

Other ideas...

Timelines

Students could produce a timeline of events to display on the wall or across the classroom. These events could include the discovery of the planets, the change in theories of the solar system, landings on the Moon, etc.

Name that Star

Stars are often given numbers for names, but what would you call them if you had a chance?

Myths and Legends

Ask students to produce a table to show all the names that the Sun, Moon and Stars have in other cultures.

Presentation

Display the fact files produced about the scientists, or the timeline produced above.

At home

What can the students see in the night sky at home? Can they identify any stars or constellations?

Plenary

Students can model their telescopes for each other.

Students could also share an interesting fact about the scientists they researched for their fact cards.

New International Edition

Unit 6: The Earth and beyond – Night and day

The objectives for this lesson are that students should be able to:

- Understand that the Earth spins on its axis as it moves around the Sun and how long it takes to spin

- Find out what directions the Sun rises and sets in, generally

- Record sunrise and sunset times for a month and present their findings

- Explain how sunrise and sunset times change during the year.

SB pp.74–75

Starter

- Look at the photograph of a sunset in the *Student Book. What time did you get up this morning? Was it light? When will you go to bed? Will it be dark then?*

- *When are the 'longest and shortest days'?* (In fact, it is the length of the daylight time that changes – the length of a 'day' is always 24 hours.) Elicit the students' ideas about why the length of daylight changes throughout the year.

- Discuss length of day and Ramadan. Why do people rise before sunrise? Why do people welcome sunset?

- Share some images of sundials and discuss their history, as a way of telling time in the past, because there weren't any watches. You could bring in the idea of clocks that were run on 'water flow' and ask what would be the things you need to be able to keep time, i.e. a regular movement of something like a steady flow of water, or the movement of the Sun.

Explain

Day and night

Use this as a revision exercise to securely fix in the students' minds how the Earth spinning causes day and night.

Sunrise, sunset

The Earth spins clockwise from west to east, so the Sun seems to move from east to west.

Use a torch and a globe with a card figure stuck on it to show how the Earth spins in and out of daylight. Ask the students to form a circle looking outwards. They should move in the circle a step at a time anticlockwise in the direction the Earth moves. Use an OHP light or desk lamp to represent the Sun. As the circle rotates they should see the Sun on their left (east/dawn), then directly in front of them (overhead at noon), then as they move on, the Sun will be on their right-hand side (west/dusk) and eventually they won't be able to see the light at all (night).

Things to do

Daylight diary

Record

Display the students' graphs alongside questions that can be answered by them.

Support

Students can draw this information as a bar chart rather than a line graph if they are completing the activity independently. Some help may be needed for a line graph. Alternatively, students could record a diary of what a typical winter day would include and compare this with a typical summer day. The diary should include the time they get up and whether or not it's light, what the temperature is like and when it gets dark.

Extend

Many diaries and almanacs have details of yearly sunrise and sunset times. Students should take an average sunrise and sunset time for a month and plot these two figures on a graphing program. They should notice a bulge in the summer months between the sunrise and sunset indicating the daylight hours are lengthening.

Day and night on other planets

All planets in our solar system behave in a similar way to the Earth. They all spin on an axis and have day and night.

Planet	Length of Astronomical day	Rounded figures
Mercury	58.65 days	59 days
Venus	243.01 days	243 days
Earth	24 hrs	1 day
Mars	24 hrs 37 min	25 hours
Jupiter	9 hrs 55 min	10 hours
Saturn	10 hrs 39 min	11 hours
Uranus	17 hrs 14 min	17 hours
Neptune	16 hrs 7 min	16 hours

Record

The students could create a solar system database and add the new data they have discovered.

Support

Round up the hours and days of the planets' orbits to make calculations easier. Reinforce that a planetary day means that the planet spins around once on its axis. Use a globe or a ball marked with a line or an 'X' so that students can easily see what 'one turn' means.

Extend

Ask the students to use secondary sources to find out more planetary facts. Venus has a longer day than it does a year. This is because Venus rotates on its axis very slowly and so its day is slightly longer than the time taken for it to orbit the Sun – its year. Make a 'fascinating fact file' to share with the class.

Dig deeper

The students have the opportunity to find the length of day and night. The length varies depending on the tilt of the Earth. As the hemispheres are tilted in different directions their daylight time varies. Countries on the equator have very little variation in daylight times.

I wonder...

The days are longer in summer due to the tilt of the Earth's axis. In summer, the Earth spends more of the day facing the Sun.

Did you know?

In some parts of the world the Earth is tilted so much towards the Sun that the land is in virtually constant daylight in the summer.

Other ideas

Time for a holiday!

Have any of the students travelled abroad for a holiday? They would need to alter the time on their watches. Ask them to find out about time zones and the International Date Line (180° longitude). Ask the students to look at holiday brochures to see if they can find the time zone of their holiday destination.

First impressions

Sunrises and sunsets have proved inspirational to many artists over the centuries. Show the students examples then let them make their own painting of dawn or dusk.

ICT ideas

Use the Internet to explore the NASA website.

At home

WS 60

Ask the students to make a collection of words to describe time. Some might be connected to the movement of objects in space like month or year; others could be hours or seconds. How many ways can we find to describe time?

Students to complete WS 60.

Plenary

Make a class mind map of what the students have learned so far.

101

Unit 6: The Earth and beyond – The Moon

The objectives for this lesson are that students should be able to:

- Understand how we can see the Moon, even though it is not a source of light

- Find out how long it takes the Moon to orbit the Earth

- Demonstrate how the Moon appears to change shape as it orbits the Earth and the Earth spins

- Make a pictorial record of the shape of the Moon every night for a month.

SB pp.76–77 | Starter

- Display a picture of the Moon. *What do we know about the Moon? Is it really made of green cheese? Is there a man in the Moon? Is the Moon a source of light?*

- Now is your opportunity to have fun with your class! Tell the students you've noticed your hands getting furry every month or so. Explain that in some countries legends say that some people turn into werewolves when there is a full Moon.

- Ask students to write questions about the Moon on sticky notes and stick these around a picture of the Moon on your wall. Explain that as they learn more about the Moon the students will be able to remove their questions as they find the answers to them.

Explain

Moonshine

It is important for students to recognize that although the Moon appears as a very bright object in our sky, it has no light of its own. The Moon is not a source of light. Rather, in common with the planets, it reflects the light from the Sun. It is reflected light we see when we see the Moon in its different phases.

The Moon's phases

As the Moon orbits the Earth, different parts of it are illuminated by the Sun. It appears that the Moon is changing shape. We call these regular changes the phases of the Moon.

The Moon's orbit

As the Moon orbits the Earth it is also spinning on its own axis. It takes 28 days to make one spin – the same time as it takes to make a full orbit of the Earth. This is why we only ever see one face of the Moon.

Sit one student in the centre (Earth) and ask another student to step sideways in a circle slowly around them, always keeping their face turned towards them. As the student walks, point out that he has in fact turned around too – think about the direction he was initially looking at and where he is facing half-way around the orbit.

Changing faces

The Moon follows a regular, predictable pattern:

- New Moon = the Sun illuminates the far side of the Moon. The Moon appears in darkness to us because none of its visible surface (the side facing Earth) is lit;

- Waxing crescent = the illuminated part of the Moon that we can see is getting bigger;

- Half Moon = during the first quarter, half of the side of the Moon facing us has sunlight falling on it and half is in darkness;

- Waxing gibbous = almost the whole of the face is lit up. Gibbous is from the Latin word meaning 'hump-backed';

- Full Moon = when all of the side of the Moon facing us is lit up;

- Waning gibbous = between full Moon and last quarter. Waning means getting smaller;

- Half Moon = the last quarter has half the Moon illuminated again – but this time the other half;

- Waning Crescent = the last sliver of Moon.

Things to do   WS 61

Model the Moon

As this activity progresses students should see more of the white half of the ball come into view as it 'waxes', then less as it wanes'.

Record

Students could make up a myth or story about how the Moon changes shape and make these into a class book alongside the scientific explanations.

Support

Make sure that the students understand what this model represents. The Moon isn't really half black and half white, it's just painted that way to show that half of the Moon is always illuminated and half always in darkness – we can't always see all of it.

Extend

Ask students to write and illustrate a short entry for a students' encyclopaedia to explain to younger students why the Moon appears to change shape.

Moon diary

The Moon rises at different times in the evening so it may not be possible for students to see it every night.

Record

Enlarge photocopies of the phases of the Moon to surround your classroom walls. Turn the coloured in phases into a flip book.

Support

Ask students to use WS 61 to record the shape of the Moon over a 28-day period.

Extend

Students draw what they see each night and note what time they see the Moon and its position in the sky.

I wonder...

The movement of the Moon is responsible for our tides on Earth. There are two high tides and two low tides every day. The Moon's gravity (and to a lesser extent the Sun's) pulls the waters of the oceans towards it and makes the waters bulge into a high tide. As the Moon orbits the Earth it causes the bulges in the ocean water to move across the Earth too, affecting each beach twice a day.

Dig deeper

Students can find information on Neil Armstrong and the first Moon landing by looking on the Internet. Emphasize the significance of this event. Reproduction newspapers often include the landing.

Did you know?

The facts illustrate the distance of the Moon from Earth and what conditions are like there.

Other ideas

Create a crater

The Moon's surface is covered with craters; many are millions of years old. They formed when meteorites, bits of space rock or pieces of comets, or asteroids, crashed into the Moon's surface.

Fill a tray with flour and dust a layer of black or grey powder paint over the surface. Try dropping different balls onto the tray from various heights. Their impact should make a crater just like on the Moon. *Which balls make the deepest craters? Why?*

Map the Moon

Students could use binoculars to look at the Moon; the features are best observed during the phases rather than at the full Moon. Remember, you can sometimes see the Moon in the daytime.

ICT ideas

Ask students to pretend they were newspaper reporters in 1969 and to create the front page of a newspaper telling the world about the first Moon landing.

Presentation

Encourage the students to make a timeline of the history of human exploration of the Moon. Ensure they include events such as Russia's spacecraft Luna 2 hitting the Moon in 1959, Luna 10 orbiting the Moon in 1966, the six Apollo Moon landings and the first woman in space.

At home

WS 62

Ask students to complete WS 62.

Plenary

Mount pictures of the phases of the Moon around your classroom and play, in teams, a 'corners' game to revise the various phases, i.e. shout out 'waxing gibbous' and the students have to find the correct picture.

103

Unit 6: The Earth and beyond – The passing year

The objectives for this lesson are that students should be able to:

- Discover what one complete orbit of the Sun by a planet is called
- Understand what a leap year is and why it is needed
- Find out how long the Earth takes to orbit the Sun
- Design and make calendar pages, using ICT.

SB pp.78–79

Starter

- Take in a photograph of your family and share it with the students. Talk about your family and their ages and birthdays. Now introduce a photograph of your mother (or brother or aunt). *She/he is only twelve years old. She's only had twelve birthdays. How can that be?*

Explain

WS 63

Happy birthday

The Sun's gravity pulls everything in the solar system towards it. The planets stay in orbit around the Sun, however, because their constant movement and speed balances out the Sun's pull of them. The effects of the Sun's gravity decrease with distance; the further away from the Sun a planet is, the slower it travels and the longer it takes to orbit. The planets all follow individual paths around the Sun. They all travel in the same direction but at different speeds. The outer planets also have a lot further to travel in their orbits.

To demonstrate how an orbit speeds up as it gets smaller, tie a small ball to the top of a pole or stick with string. Hold the ball high up and let it swing into orbit around the pole. As the string winds around the pole and the ball's orbit decreases you should see it get faster.

Leap years

The Earth completes its orbit around the Sun once every 365 and a quarter days. This gives us our Earth year of 365 days with the extra quarter days adding up every four years to give us a leap year – a year incorporating an extra day (29 February) into the calendar.

The seasons

Seasons occur because the Earth is tilted, not because the Earth gets close to the Sun in the summer.

As the Earth moves around the Sun, for part of the time the northern half is tilted towards the Sun and the southern half is tilted away from the Sun. Consequently, the northern half gets stronger sunlight – the sunlight is more intense making the temperature rise because it is shining more directly on a smaller area, the Sun is higher in the sky and there is daylight for longer.

Six months later, the Earth has moved to the other side of the Sun and the northern hemisphere is tilted away from the Sun. The sunlight is spread out over a wider area, the Sun is lower in the sky and the daylight hours are reduced giving colder temperatures and more wind.

Some places near the equator have two seasons, often known as the rainy and the dry seasons. The Hindu calendar has six seasons.

Demonstrate this using a globe and a torch with a strong beam.

Things to do

WS 64

How the Earth travels

This activity will allow the students to show that they understand that the Earth is spinning on its axis as it orbits the Sun creating day, night and the year. It will need co-ordination and communication on the part of the students with each other, especially to carry out the narration to explain what the 'play' is modelling.

The students can complete WS 64 to reinforce their learning.

Make a calendar

This activity reinforces the changes of the seasons and the number facts connected with the movement of the Earth. Take in as many calendars as you can. What are the common features?

Record

Display some of the calendar pages on the walls. Get the students to make up questions that can be answered by their calendars and display these.

Support

As the students illustrate the months, encourage them to include seasonal features and captions, explaining why the seasons change or what the temperatures or hours of daylight should be.

Extend

Students could design a calendar for another planet. Would the seasons be very different there? How many days would be in a year?

I wonder...

WS
65

In many countries, it is hotter in summer than in winter because of the tilt of the Earth's axis. The days are longer in summer as the relevant hemisphere spends more of the day facing the Sun. The Earth receives more energy here and so the weather gets hotter. The Sun is higher in the sky in the summer and so the Sun's energy is more direct and concentrated into a smaller area than in the winter. This too raises the temperature.

In the winter, the northern hemisphere is tilted away from the Sun, the daylight hours are shorter and the sunlight is more scattered over a larger surface area. This makes for cooler temperatures.

As the equator is at the same angle towards the Sun throughout the year, there is little seasonal change.

Ask the students to complete WS 65.

Dig deeper

Use the Internet to research the way the seasons affect animals. Link migration with the changes in temperature across the hemispheres.

Did you know?

These facts illustrate some of the effects caused by the Earth's tilted axis.

Other ideas

Food for a season

Ask students to research seasonal food. Which foods were traditionally available in the summer and which in the winter months? What did people do if they wanted fruit or vegetables 'out of season' before the advent of refrigeration and air travel? Which plants only flower in the spring or in the autumn?

Draw an ellipse

The planets orbit the Sun in a shape called an ellipse. The shape is like a slightly squashed circle, although most of the planetary orbits are virtually circular. The orbits of Mercury and Mars are the most elliptical. The solar system is arranged like a flat disc with the planets' orbits one inside the other on the same plane.

Presentation

Ask students to make a display of how the changing seasons are reflected in their local environment.

At home

We have 12 months in the year. Ask students to find out more about why the months are named as they are. *Which months are named after Roman emperors?*

Plenary

The students should now be able to explain why your relation has had so few birthdays. They were, of course, born on 29 February. If the students had been born on this day, how old would they be now?

Get the students to research the origins of the names of the months in their local calendar.

Unit 6: The Earth and beyond – Unit 6: Review

The objectives for this lesson are that students should be able to:

- Check what they have learned about the Earth and beyond in this Unit

- Find out how they are working towards, within and beyond the Grade 5 level.

Outcomes

Students working towards Grade 5 level will:

- Recognize that the Earth, Sun and Moon are spherical and describe how shadows change as the Sun appears to move across the sky.

- Recognize that we have day and night that is caused by the Earth spinning.

In addition, students working within Grade 5 level will:

- Communicate clearly the evidence to support that the Earth, Sun and Moon are spherical.

- Explain in terms of the rotation of the Earth why shadows change and the Sun appears to move across the sky during the course of the day.

- Recognize that a day is 24 hours.

- Recognize that it is daylight in the part of the Earth facing the Sun.

- Recognize that the Moon orbits the Earth.

- Identify patterns in secondary data about sunrise and sunset.

- Make careful observations and collect enough evidence to test their ideas.

- Present data in bar charts and begin to use line graphs independently.

- Recognize how scientists have used creative thinking to suggest new ideas.

Further to this, students working beyond Grade 5 level will also:

- Explain that the changes in the appearance of the Moon over a period of 28 days arise from the Moon orbiting the Earth once every 28 days.

- Model how the Earth travels through space.

- Independently represent times of sunrise and sunset in graphs.

- Use their results to draw conclusions, explaining and communicating them clearly.

Check-up

Solar eclipses are less common than lunar eclipses; they happen twice a year but most are partial eclipses, when the Moon passes in front of the Sun but does not cover all of it. In a complete solar eclipse the Sun, Moon and Earth line up directly so that the Moon casts a shadow on the Earth's surface. The far side of the Moon is lit by the Sun in a solar eclipse so it appears dark to us, as the side facing us is unlit.

Assessment   WS 66   WS 67

Use the Unit 6 assessments on WSs 66 and 67 to check the students' understanding of the content of the Unit. The answers are given opposite.

Name: _____ Date: _____

WS 66 Unit 6 assessment 1

1 Safia is making a model. Tick (✓) the three best objects she could use to represent the Earth, Sun and Moon.

cushion ☐   tissue box ☐   football ☐
ping-pong ball ☐   tennis ball ☐   beach ball ☐
rugby ball ☐   poppy seed ☐   roll of tape ☐
small coin ☐

2 How many times does the Earth spin on its axis each day? Circle the correct answer.

1   7   24   28   365

3 Write true or false after each of these sentences.

a) The Earth orbits the Sun. _____
b) The Moon orbits the Earth. _____
c) The Sun orbits the Earth. _____
d) The planets orbit the Earth. _____

4 a) Use the names Sun, Moon and Earth to label the diagram.

B _____   C _____
A _____

b) How long does it take A to orbit C? _____
c) How long does it take B to orbit A? _____

66   Heinemann Explore Science Grade 5

The answer!

The Unit begins with the problem of Vijay and the disappearing star. The star hasn't really disappeared, of course, but the Earth has moved in relation to it so it appears to be in a different place – in this case behind his house and out of his sight.

And finally...

A trip to a planetarium or observatory would round off this topic perfectly.

Answers

Unit 6 assessment 1

1 tennis ball or ping-pong ball, beach ball and poppy seed

2 1

3 **a** true **b** true **c** false **d** false

4 **a** A Earth, B Moon, C Sun

   b 365 and a quarter days or 365 days approximately

   c 28 days approximately

Unit 6 assessment 2

5 Accept any explanation that mentions that although the Sun appears to change position it is the Earth spinning on its axis which causes the shadows to change. Although it may look as if the Sun is moving from east to west, it is the Earth that is moving.

6 **a** The side away from the Sun.

   b night

   c Accept any point on the curve of the Earth on the side of the Sun.

107